GW00360080

David Symes left [...]
degree in microbiolog[...]
been working in pub[...]
has been freelance [...]
health subjects. He has written one other book, *Cholesterol – Reducing Your Risk*, also written in association with the FHA.

Annette Zakary studied at Robert Gordon's Institute of Technology in Aberdeen, gaining a BSc in nutrition and dietetics. After undertaking practical training in a London and Sussex hospital, and industrial training at the Rowett Research Institute, Aberdeen, she took exams leading to her State Registration in Dietetics. She has been working with the FHA as their dietitian/counsellor since 1989, and is also an active member of the British Dietetic Association.

The **Family Heart Association** is a charity helping the public, industry and the medical profession to fight heart disease. Your help is needed to ensure that the work goes on:

- To have cholesterol screening widely available.
- To set up a family information service offering advice to those wishing to adopt a low cholesterol lifestyle.
- To help industry set up employee screening and counselling programmes.
- To raise awareness of the dangers of high cholesterol and other risk factors for heart disease.
- To provide cholesterol screening to enable those with inherited conditions and others at high risk of heart disease to be discovered and treated.

THE FAMILY HEART ASSOCIATION

LOW–FAT DIET BOOK

David Symes and Annette Zakary

POSITIVE HEALTH GUIDE

© The Family Heart Association, David Symes and Annette Zakary
1991

First published in 1991 by
Macdonald Optima, a division of
Macdonald & Co. (Publishers) Ltd

A member of Maxwell Macmillan Pergamon Publishing Corporation

British Library Cataloguing in Publication Data
Symes, David
  The Family Heart Association low-fat diet book.
  1. Food: Low fat dishes – Recipes
  I. Title   II. Zakary, Annette
  641.5638

  ISBN 0–356–20043–4

Macdonald & Co. (Publishers) Ltd
Orbit House
1 New Fetter Lane
London EC4A 1AR

Typeset in Times by Leaper & Gard Ltd, Bristol

Printed and bound in Great Britain by
Cox & Wyman Ltd, Reading

CONTENTS

Acknowledgments

ACKNOWLEDGMENTS

First of all our grateful thanks go to Melissa Brooks, who was instrumental in dreaming up the initial idea and who came up with a number of useful suggestions along the way.

Suzy Powling was not only responsible for various other suggestions, but also helped to write bits of Chapter 5. Furthermore, she brought her considerable skills as a cookery editor to bear on the manuscript as a whole during its editing.

Various people contributed ideas and suggestions for the recipes, including M. Anton Mosimann, Melissa Brooks, Suzy Powling, Mrs Sass Tyson, Mrs Lyn Enos, Mrs Annemarie Bishop, Mrs Joan Dodd and Mrs Marion Symes.

We would like to thank all the staff at the FHA for their encouragement and consideration shown during the writing of this book, and would particularly like to thank Tom Sanders, not only for his foreword to the book but also for the loan of his computer software to aid the nutritional analysis of the recipes.

The diagram on page 20 is based on a similar chart in *Treat Obesity Seriously*, by John S. Garrow (Churchill Livingstone).

Last, and by no means least, our thanks are due to Harriet Griffey at Macdonald Optima, without whom this book would not be possible.

1

INTRODUCTION

'Not another diet-based recipe book' you might be heard to groan as you flick through the pages of this book. 'So what's so different about this one?'

Well, there are two very important differences.

- This book encourages you to eat hearty sensible-sized meals and still reduce your weight if you are overweight. By cutting down on the proportion of fat in your diet you can increase the other constituents of your diet and still lose weight.
- By reducing the quantity of fat, and particularly of saturated fat, that you consume you will also reduce your risk of heart disease – the number one killer disease in the Western world.

REDUCE YOUR WEIGHT, NOT YOUR MEALS

In the Western world, in general, we eat too much and take too little exercise. Furthermore, our affluence has enabled us to afford rich and generally fatty foods that compound the problem. The result is that a high proportion of people are overweight. Some are only slightly overweight; a few are grossly obese; and many want to lose weight.

1

In this book we will show you that fat – an overall term for all the edible fats and oils – is, perhaps not surprisingly, the most fattening food we eat. In more technical terms, it is much more energy-dense than protein and carbohydrate. What this means, therefore, is that if you can reduce the fat content of your diet and instead make more use of carbohydrates to fill you up, you will take in less calories (or joules), i.e. less energy. And if you take in less energy you will gradually tend to come down to your natural weight.

Now, this is a very easy statement to make, but how do you go about preparing meals that are low in fat but still tasty and interesting, and which look appetising? Theory is one thing, but how do you go about putting it into practice? In this book we give you a wealth of recipes – everything from sandwiches and snacks to full-blown gourmet meals – that are low in fat but high in taste and interest.

REDUCE THE FAT, REDUCE THE HEART DISEASE

Many people – perhaps most – when asked what the principal killer disease is in the UK, would probably answer cancer. However, distressing though cancer is, it is not the chief killer. Nor are car accidents. Nor is AIDS. By far and away the leading cause of death in the UK is coronary heart disease – the clogging up of the arteries that leads to heart attacks.

If we look at the statistics in more detail, they make for grim reading. For example, in the late 1980s about 180,000 people a year were dying of heart disease in the UK; that's nearly 500 people a day, or about one every two-and-a-half minutes. Within the UK population one in three men and one in four women will die as a result of coronary heart disease. It has been described, and rightly so, as a killer of epidemic proportions.

How does the UK compare with other countries? Is this

2

scourge of heart disease a global phenomenon? Yes and no. Coronary heart disease is a major killer in countries around the world, but not in all countries. With a few exceptions, it strikes in those nations that have Westernised cultures and lifestyles, particularly in the countries of northern and eastern Europe, north America and Australia and New Zealand.

But all is not quite so gloomy as it might be. In the late 1960s it began to be realised that action could be taken to lower these rampaging death rates, and since then some countries have seen dramatic drops in deaths from heart disease, notably the US, Canada, Finland, Australia and New Zealand.

These reductions in death rates were not chance events. They indicate that people were beginning to understand better the causes of coronary heart disease and were starting to act on this knowledge. For example, it was realised that the sedentary Western lifestyle was a major problem – if you sat at a desk all day and took little or no exercise, you increased your chances of heart disease. People began to take more exercise and the jogging boom and the physical fitness crazes took off. People also began to look at other areas of their lives, like smoking.

It also became apparent that diet played a significant part in increasing the risk of heart disease. A rich fatty diet not only tends to make you overweight; it also tends to raise the level of cholesterol in your bloodstream and, as our knowledge of the processes surrounding the onset of coronary heart disease became ever more sophisticated, it was revealed that raised cholesterol levels in the bloodstream were a very strong predictor of subsequent heart disease. People therefore began to modify their diets, reducing their overall intake of fat, if possible substituting vegetable fat for animal fat, and eating more fruit and vegetables.

And so we return to the point made in the previous section – eat less fat and concentrate more on carbohydrates, the major constituent of fruit and vegetables. To this end, not only are the recipes in this book tasty, nutritious and designed to help you keep your weight down to a sensible level; they are also designed to keep your blood cholesterol level within healthy limits and thus help you reduce your risks of heart disease.

ENERGY VALUES OF FOOD

All food contains energy. This is why we eat; the food we eat provides us with energy, which we then expend on our daily activities.

The kilocalorie (Kcal) is a convenient measure of the amount of energy contained within a substance. Taken literally, it indicates the amount of energy that substance would liberate if it was burned as a fuel. It ought to be noted at the outset that kilocalories are often abbreviated to calories or Calories; strictly speaking, this is an incorrect terminology, but it is something that is probably too ingrained in the public's mind to change overnight. A more recent measure of the energy content of food is the kilojoule (kJ) or megajoule (MJ); 1 kilocalorie is 4.2 kJ, and 1,000 kilocalories are 4.2 MJ.

Our food is our fuel, so in the case of food the kilocalorie gives a measure of the amount of chemical energy that can be released after the food has been eaten and broken down within the body. High-calorie foods are thus those foods that are energy-dense, meaning that much energy will be released from relatively small amounts once they have been broken down within the body. And the purpose of this book is to provide you with a bank of recipes and ideas for meals that will be low in energy-dense ingredients, i.e. low in fat.

HOW TO USE THIS BOOK

The first part of this book – Chapters 2 to 4 – explains the basis of the low-fat diet and how it will help you control your weight and lower your risk of heart disease.

The second part of the book – Chapters 5 to 13 – consists of the recipes themselves, plus a wealth of advice, tips, a typical week's menu and a shopping list for this menu.

Each recipe gives you the ingredients in both imperial and metric measures. Furthermore, at the end of each recipe we give an indication of how many servings you will get from that recipe, what the fat content of each serving will be, and what the energy content of each serving will be. Those who want to lose weight need to take into consideration both the energy content and the fat content of a dish; those who are merely concerned with lowering their risk of heart disease will probably be more concerned with the fat content.

2

WHAT ARE FATS?

Before discussing low-fat diets and low-fat recipes, it might be as well to determine exactly what fats are. If the broad principle is to cut down on the fat content of the diet, we need to know what areas of the diet will be affected.

THE CONSTITUENTS OF THE DIET

At its very simplest, food can be considered to consist of the following:

- Carbohydrate.
- Protein.
- Fat.
- Other nutrients.
- Fibre.

Food also contains water, to a greater or lesser extent, but this need not concern us too much here as it has no nutritional value.

Carbohydrate

Carbohydrate consists of the elements carbon, hydrogen and oxygen, and is used largely as an energy source. During the process of digestion, dietary carbohydrate is

6

broken down into small units in the gut. These units are known generally as sugars, the best known of which is glucose. What we know and buy as sugar – the sugar you get in bags in the shops – is correctly known as sucrose, and consists of two simple sugars, or units, called glucose and fructose.

Nutritionists distinguish between simple and complex carbohydrate:

- **Simple carbohydrate** is invariably found in highly refined and processed foods. These foods tend to consist of little or nothing else but carbohydrate, sugar (sucrose) being the best example. Simple carbohydrate is quickly broken down into simple sugars in the gut, from where they flood into the bloodstream. Typical examples of simple carbohydrates, in addition to sugar, are syrup, honey, white bread, bought cakes and biscuits, and sweets.
- **Complex carbohydrate** is found in the less refined foods. In these foods the carbohydrate consists of a wider range of building blocks, and they are combined with other nutrients. In the gut, complex carbohydrate therefore tends to be broken down much more slowly than simple carbohydrate. Typical examples of complex carbohydrate are wholemeal bread, breakfast cereals, fruit, vegetables and pulses.

Once carbohydrate has been broken down in the gut into its basic building blocks, these units pass into the bloodstream and are then transported around the body and used as energy sources wherever they are needed; in other words, they are the fuel that the body needs in order to function. However, if we take in too much of this fuel it is ultimately laid down as fat – the fat is simply an energy store.

Protein
The protein in our food provides us with the basic building blocks for our body; it is intimately involved in the

7

maintenance and repair of old cells and in the manufacture of new cells. Protein largely consists of the elements carbon, hydrogen, oxygen and nitrogen, with traces of other elements incorporated into various different protein structures. These elements are linked together to form the amino acids – the basic units of protein structure – and, in turn, different combinations and numbers of amino acids are linked together to construct the many different proteins. When we digest protein it is broken down into its constituent amino acid units, which are then absorbed from the gut, processed and used in different parts of the body as and where necessary.

From this it should be apparent that it is essential that you consume enough protein – if you don't you are likely to suffer from malnutrition. But most people don't need as much protein in their diet as they think; and if you consume an excess of protein, the surplus amino acids are merely utilised as fuel to give energy. Certainly in the West we are used to consuming far more protein than we need. The only other detail that we need to know about protein is the distinction between high and low biological value proteins (often called first and second class proteins). The human body can actually synthesise many of the amino acids itself, but not all of them. The amino acids it can't manufacture are the essential amino acids, so called because it is essential that we obtain them from our diet.

- **High biological value protein**, derived from animals and animal products, is a rich source of essential amino acids, and contains them in the right proportions for our use.
- **Low biological value protein**, derived from plants, does not contain these essential amino acids in the correct proportions for human needs; to survive merely on plant produce is perfectly feasible, as evidenced by vegans, but you need to take in a combination of low biological value protein in order to ensure the correct balance of the essential amino acids.

8

Fat

Like carbohydrate, fat also consists of the elements carbon, hydrogen and oxygen, but in different proportions. In fact it is more accurate to refer to this group as lipids, of which the fats and oils are merely a subgroup. The only other lipid that need concern us here, however, is cholesterol. And don't be put off by the distinction between oils and fats; they are roughly the same thing, except that fats are solid at room temperature and oils are liquid.

The great majority of the fat we consume each day has the same basic structure, each molecule consisting of:

- A three-pronged backbone.
- Attached to each prong of this backbone is a unit of what are called fatty acids.

This is called a triglyceride structure, and is found throughout the range of fats and oils. The three-pronged backbone to the molecule always remains the same, but

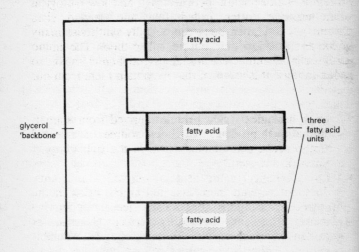

Basic structure of a triglyceride

9

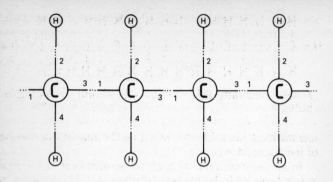

(C) — carbon atom

(H) — hydrogen atom

Bonding arrangement between carbon atoms in a fatty acid

the fatty acids attached to this backbone can vary widely, conferring different properties on the fats and oils.

A fatty acid is basically a string of carbon atoms joined together. Each carbon atom in the string has the ability to form four links with other atoms. In a chain-like molecule such as a fatty acid it should be apparent that one of these links will be with the carbon atom to the right in the chain and another will be with the carbon atom to the left in the chain. This leaves two links, or bonds, left over, and in most cases these will be mopped up by hydrogen atoms. Such a structure is called a *saturated* fatty acid, as it is saturated with hydrogen atoms, i.e. it can take up no more; a saturated fatty acid is thus a string of carbon atoms with two hydrogen atoms bristling off each carbon atom.

In some fatty acids, though, not all the bonds coming off the carbon atoms in the chain are mopped up by hydrogen atoms; in these fatty acids, adjacent carbon atoms in the chain are linked by two bonds. Where this occurs the carbon atoms only have one bond left over for a hydrogen atom, and the fatty acid is described as being

```
       H  H  H  H  H  H  H  H  H  H  H  H  H  H  H  H  H
       |  |  |  |  |  |  |  |  |  |  |  |  |  |  |  |  |
H  —  C— C— C— C— C— C— C— C— C— C— C— C— C— C— C— C— C— COOH
       |  |  |  |  |  |  |  |  |  |  |  |  |  |  |  |  |
       H  H  H  H  H  H  H  H  H  H  H  H  H  H  H  H  H
```

A saturated fatty acid, stearic acid, found for example in butter

unsaturated, i.e. it has not taken up the maximum number of hydrogen atoms.

In an unsaturated fatty acid, by no means all the carbon atoms form such double bonds; there are usually only one or a few.

```
      H  H  H  H  H  H  H  H        H  H  H  H  H  H  H
      |  |  |  |  |  |  |  |        |  |  |  |  |  |  |
H  —  C— C— C— C— C— C— C— C— C= C— C— C— C— C— C— C— C— COOH
      |  |  |  |  |  |  |  |        |  |  |  |  |  |  |
      H  H  H  H  H  H  H  H        H  H  H  H  H  H  H
```

A mono-unsaturated fatty acid, oleic acid, found for example in olive oil

```
      H  H  H  H  H  H      H  H      H  H  H  H  H  H  H
      |  |  |  |  |  |      |  |      |  |  |  |  |  |  |
H  —  C— C— C— C— C— C= C— C— C= C— C— C— C— C— C— C— C— COOH
      |  |  |  |  |        |  |      |  |  |  |  |  |  |
      H  H  H  H  H        H  H      H  H  H  H  H  H  H
```

A polyunsaturated fatty acid, linoleic acid, found for example in sunflower oil

```
      H  H  H      H  H      H  H      H  H  H  H  H  H  H
      |  |  |      |  |      |  |      |  |  |  |  |  |  |
H  —  C— C— C= C— C— C= C— C— C= C— C— C— C— C— C— C— C— COOH
      |  |        |  |      |  |      |  |  |  |  |  |  |
      H  H        H  H      H  H      H  H  H  H  H  H  H
```

Another polyunsaturated fatty acid, linolenic acid, found for example in soya oil

- If there is only one such double bond, the fatty acid is understandably described as mono-unsaturated – it is a **mono-unsaturated fatty acid** or a **MUFA**.
- If there is more than one such double bond it is described as polyunsaturated – it is a **polyunsaturated fatty acid** or a **PUFA**.

When we eat some fat it is broken down in the gut into its subunits – the fatty acids and the three-pronged backbone – and these then pass across the gut wall into the bloodstream. Once in the bloodstream they are transported around the body, to be used as sources of energy or to be laid down as energy stores – i.e. as fat – if they are not needed immediately.

Other nutrients

Nutritionally, this category is very important as it covers such broad groups of nutrients as:

- Vitamins.
- Minerals.
- Micronutrients, i.e. the trace elements.

All of these are essential constituents of the diet.

Fibre

Much has been written about fibre in the last few years. The irony is that fibre is not a nutrient at all. Its very definition conveys the fact that we don't digest fibre – it is not broken down and absorbed into the body. Instead it passes out of the digestive tract in largely the same form in which it is taken in.

Having said that, fibre is very important. Food, and the subsequent residues of digestion, are moved along the digestive tract by a sort of muscular squeezing action. If we eat no fibre the food mass has little bulk to it – it's just a slushy mush – and this muscular squeezing action has nothing much to work on. The result is that the food and its residues take far too long to pass through the digestive system, and various digestive and digestive-related disorders can result. Fibre is therefore essential in our diet; it provides bulk and gives something for the digestive tract to grip on as it squeezes the food mass along.

Fibre is a component of the complex carbohydrate group. Fibre is not a single entity but comprises a whole range of substances. In particular, we have realised that there are two very distinct sorts of fibre, and as we shall discover, it is very important to distinguish between them.

- **Insoluble fibre**. This is relatively inert but is important as it adds rough bulk to the food mass. It absorbs water whilst passing through our intestines, making the food mass softer and easier to expel from our bodies. Insoluble fibre is provided by many whole cereals such as wheat, rye and barley – wheat bran is perhaps the best known.
- **Soluble fibre**. This is a softer sort of fibre, and has the important characteristic of being able to dissolve in water. This slows the rate at which foods pass into the stomach and are digested. Most fruit and vegetables contain soluble fibre, as do the pulses like lentils, chickpeas, red beans and so on. Whole oats are also a rich source of soluble fibre, of which oat bran contains the largest proportion.

CHOLESTEROL

What is it?

We have already mentioned cholesterol briefly when discussing fats. Fats, you will remember, are the major dietary constituent of a larger group, called the lipids, and cholesterol is another member of the lipid group. If you obtained a solid block of cholesterol you would see that it is white and waxy, and quite soft at room temperature. Much of the cholesterol in the human body is incorporated into complex structures. It can also occur in fat particles circulating in the bloodstream; if the quantity of these

13

cholesterol-rich fatty particles in the blood gets too great, the cholesterol can then be laid down as white deposits on the lining of the arteries.

What does cholesterol do?

Many people are now aware of some of the rudiments of a healthy diet; they realise that we need to reduce the amount of fat we consume, and some will tell you that high levels of cholesterol in the diet are a bad thing. From this you might conclude that cholesterol itself is a bad thing, and that we'd be better off without it. Not true. A limited amount of cholesterol is vitally important to the functioning of our bodies.

Cholesterol is involved in a number of functions within the human body. It is a building block for various hormones, for vitamin D and for bile, is involved in the structure and function of the brain and the nervous system, and is essential for the microscopic workings of each cell.

FATS, CHOLESTEROL AND DIET

By now you should have realised that cholesterol is an absolutely essential part of our existence, although, as we shall discover later, in excess it can be very damaging. But where does our cholesterol come from?

The majority of the cholesterol in the body is actually manufactured in the liver and the small intestine (part of the gut), as much as 1 gram a day being produced at these sites. Even if we take in no cholesterol in our diet, no dietary animal fat and only limited amounts of vegetable fat, as provided by a vegan diet, the body continues to churn out the cholesterol, with no attached risk and with no detriment to health.

Having said that, if we consume the rich diet typical in the Western world we take in a lot more fat than our body seems to be designed to cope with, particularly if we take little exercise. There are two dietary factors which may affect cholesterol levels:

- We take in large quantities of **saturated fats** – fats containing saturated fatty acids – in the form of meat, dairy produce and processed vegetable fat, such as margarine. And an excess of saturated fats in the diet results directly in an increased level of cholesterol in the bloodstream; the higher the proportion of saturated fat in the diet, the greater the risk of excess levels of cholesterol circulating in the bloodstream.
- We take in **cholesterol** in our diet, largely in the form of eggs, dairy produce and meat, particularly offal meat – liver, kidneys and so on. This dietary cholesterol should limit the amount of cholesterol the body makes, but the mechanism that controls this seems to work better in some people than others.

Of the two factors, the proportion of saturated fat in the diet seems to be of far greater importance in producing an excess of cholesterol in the system. However, as it tends to be the same dietary items that contain both saturated fats and cholesterol, reducing the proportion of saturated fat in the diet will automatically tend to reduce the amount of dietary cholesterol.

3

EATING TOO MUCH FAT

If you are reading this book it is probably because you feel
you are overweight and want to get down to a more
comfortable weight, or because you want to try to adopt a
diet for yourself and your family that will lessen the risks
of heart disease. Or maybe you are just interested in what
you think might be a healthier diet than you are
consuming at the moment.

Whatever your reasons, in this chapter we will outline
some of the excesses of the typical Western diet and some
of the problems that arise from them.

THE WESTERN DIET AND LIFESTYLE

In the Western industrialised countries we have gradually
achieved a standard of living that earlier generations –
even our grandparents – never dreamed of. Yet while this
affluent lifestyle has removed many discomforts and
solved many problems, it has brought with it its own
problems.

Too much food
To begin with, it could almost be said that we are too
affluent for our own good. Certainly most of us are able to

afford to eat as much, and more, than we want. No longer do we have to eat to live; instead, many of us now live to eat. Two or three substantial meals a day, plus snacks and sweets in between, are what everyone takes for granted; rich foods are routine parts of our everyday diet.

But such plenty is not universal, and it might come as something of a shock if we had to live for a year on the simpler and much less varied fare of someone in a less developed country, let alone in a Third World country. This is not to decry our affluence, merely to point out that the majority of the people on this planet live on far meaner fare than us.

Wringing our hands over our well-stocked kitchens and overloaded tables is one thing; trying to reduce our consumption of food is something else. The fact of the matter is that we have got used to eating too much, and in particular too much rich food. Asking people to eat less has been shown to be impractical, as evidenced by the millions of people who have tried to do so with the aim of losing weight, and failed.

For a diet to be realistic it has to start out with the basic assumption that people like eating – that is why so many people are overweight. For this reason, for any diet to work it somehow has to allow people to eat as much as they like, within reason. And that is what we have set out to do in this book.

Too much fat

Not only do we tend to eat too much food generally; we also tend to eat too many rich fatty foods. In the past, such foods would have been too expensive, or just unknown, but as food has become relatively cheaper and transport and distribution networks have become ever more sophisticated, so the food that we take for granted has come from an ever wider range. As two examples, consider the croissant and the chip.

Millions of people now take their holidays abroad, and this brings them into contact with all sorts of foods and cooking styles from different countries. An enduring

17

delight when travelling in France is being able to enjoy fresh croissants for breakfast. But now many local bakers make them, all the supermarket chains stock them, and fast-food chains are churning out stuffed croissants as fast as they can. Croissants may not be a regular feature of your diet, but they are certainly readily available.

Or consider the humble chip. Time was when you could only get chips at one shop – the fish and chippie. Gradually more cafés and restaurants began to offer them, but they were still considered something of a treat. But now they are ubiquitous: every pub, hotel and restaurant serves them as a matter of course, nearly every fast-food shop serves them, and many households have deep-fat fryers that allow chips to be served with every meal.

The croissant and the chip may seem vastly different foods, but they both have one thing in common. They both have a very high fat content. And so it is with many of the foods we take for granted today.

Maybe you don't realise quite how high the fat content of the typical Western diet is. Fatty cuts of meat, streaky bacon and chips are obviously high in fat, but what about all the rest?

- Among the meat products, sausages, luncheon meats, pâtés, meat pies and pasties, and salami all have a high fat content.
- Deep-fat-fried food is high in fat – chips, scampi and crisps, for example.
- Butter, margarine, lard, suet and the like are obviously high in fat.
- Anything made with butter, margarine and so on is therefore high in fat – cakes, pastry, biscuits and many puddings.
- Whole milk has a lot of fat in it, and cream is even higher.
- Cheese is high in fat.
- Chocolate is high in fat, as are toffee and fudge.
- Mayonnaise – watch out for it in coleslaws, ready-prepared salads and sandwiches.

18

It's quite an impressive list, isn't it, and covers many foods and ingredients that we take for granted. And it's not as if these are occasional items in our diet; they are regular features of our day-to-day eating.

Not enough exercise

This apparent over-consumption of food, and of fats in particular, would perhaps be excusable if we were constantly undertaking hard physical work. But the opposite is the case.

The manual content of many jobs – the hard physical labour – has been reduced or removed, and many other such jobs have simply disappeared, to be replaced by sedentary office jobs where we sit at desks or computer screens all day. Our transport systems have become ever more sophisticated. No longer do we rely on our feet, or a horse, or a bicycle; now we can drive anywhere and everywhere. We no longer use stairs, but ride in lifts. And even the housework has been swept away by an avalanche of labour-saving devices.

The sum total of these developments is that we take less exercise, at the very time when we are consuming more and richer food. The energy we are taking in from our food is increasing, and the energy that we are expending in our everyday lives is decreasing. Small wonder, then, that so many people are overweight.

BEING OVERWEIGHT

Many books such as this might head this section 'Obesity', which implies being extremely overweight. However, being obese is not the same thing as being overweight; being overweight is merely weighing more than a defined ideal for your height and sex. But whatever words you use, the fact of the matter is that between 30 and 50 per cent of the UK population are overweight, and between 5 and 10 per cent have a serious weight problem. What's worse is that, more and more, we are seeing fat adolescents and fat

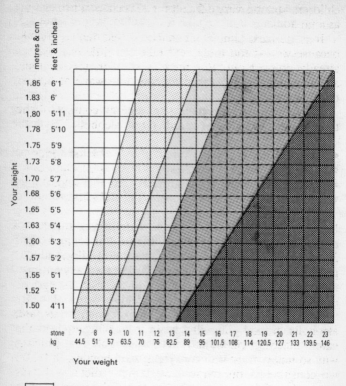

metres & cm	feet & inches
1.85	6'1
1.83	6'
1.80	5'11
1.78	5'10
1.75	5'9
1.73	5'8
1.70	5'7
1.68	5'6
1.65	5'5
1.63	5'4
1.60	5'3
1.57	5'2
1.55	5'1
1.52	5'
1.50	4'11

Your height

| stone | 7 | 8 | 9 | 10 | 11 | 12 | 13 | 14 | 15 | 16 | 17 | 18 | 19 | 20 | 21 | 22 | 23 |
| kg | 44.5 | 51 | 57 | 63.5 | 70 | 76 | 82.5 | 89 | 95 | 101.5 | 108 | 114 | 120.5 | 127 | 133 | 139.5 | 146 |

Your weight

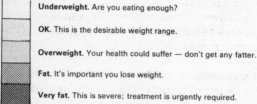

Underweight. Are you eating enough?

OK. This is the desirable weight range.

Overweight. Your health could suffer — don't get any fatter.

Fat. It's important you lose weight.

Very fat. This is severe; treatment is urgently required.

Guidelines for body weight relative to height

20

children, and it is very difficult for a fat child not to end up as a fat adult.

It is perhaps simple to conclude that this is merely because we eat too much and take too little exercise, as already pointed out. But there is another, less obvious, and more important reason for this tidal wave of fatness that is engulfing us.

Let us begin by looking at the energy content of the three major food groups, together with alcohol:

- 1 gram of fat supplies   9 kilocalories
- 1 gram of protein supplies   4 kilocalories
- 1 gram of carbohydrate supplies 3.75 kilocalories
- 1 ml of alcohol supplies   7 kilocalories

It is easy to see that, weight for weight, fats supply far more energy than all the other nutrients. For example, 100 grams (about 4oz) of fat will supply 900 kilocalories – perhaps between a quarter and a third of the daily requirement of someone in an office job. In contrast, 100 grams of carbohydrate will supply only 375 kilocalories.

What this means is that if you eat a diet rich in fats (and alcoholic drinks) you will take in a lot of energy, to the extent that you will be hard put to use it all up – which is why so many of us are overweight. And how much fat do we consume in our typical Westerner's diet? Well, for many of us the proportion is 20 per cent by weight, while for some it is higher – 25 or even 30 per cent by weight.

There are thus two features of our typical diet that will tend to lead to our being overweight:

- We eat too much.
- Of more significance, we eat too much fat.

HEART DISEASE

As was pointed out in Chapter 1, the statistics relating to coronary heart disease are very alarming, particularly as so much heart disease is preventable. But what exactly is heart disease, and how is it related to diet?

What is heart disease?

To begin at the beginning, all parts of the body need oxygen in order to function, just as a fire needs an air supply to burn. We take air into our lungs, from where it passes into the bloodstream, to be transported around the body to where it is needed. All the organs and tissues of the body also need nutrients – fuel – in order to function, and these nutrients are also transported around the body in the bloodstream. Waste products are removed from the tissues by the bloodstream and carried to the organs of excretion. Many of the functions of the immune system are carried out by constituents of the bloodstream circulating around the body. It should therefore be clear that the bloodstream is an essential transport system, carrying a wide range of products around the body.

But the blood does not dribble around the blood vessels of its own accord. It has to be pumped – and the pump has to be extremely efficient and hardworking, for it has to beat once a second or more, every second of our lives. Think of clenching and unclenching your hand every second for a few minutes, then think of doing the same thing for the rest of your life – it will give you some idea of the work the heart is doing.

The heart is constructed of muscle, and, like all muscles, it needs its own blood supply in order to provide it with oxygen and nutrients and to take away the waste products it generates. The blood vessels that supply the heart are the coronary arteries and veins, so called because as they loop around the heart they resemble a crown; the coronary arteries supply the heart with blood, oxygen and nutrients, while the coronary veins take away the blood containing the waste products. The larger coronary arteries are about the size of a large drinking-straw, but these soon subdivide to form smaller and smaller vessels that encircle and penetrate the areas of heart muscle.

When you think about the regularity and constancy of

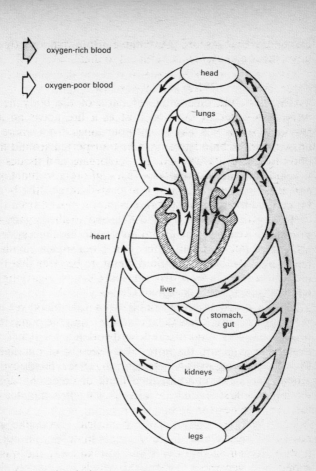

oxygen-rich blood

oxygen-poor blood

head

lungs

heart

liver

stomach, gut

kidneys

legs

The blood circulation system

the beating of the heart you will realise that any damage to
or disease of the coronary arteries will have potentially
disastrous results; if this essential fuel supply to the heart
is in any way reduced, the heart will function less and less
efficiently; blood is then pumped to the rest of the body
less effectively; and the heart complains when it is over-
worked. In short, we have coronary heart disease – disease

23

caused by the less efficient functioning of the coronary arteries of the heart.

Atherosclerosis is the fundamental problem underlying coronary heart disease, and is caused by a hard porridgey-looking deposit found sticking to the insides of the arteries. The insides of the blood vessels should be smooth and slippery so that blood can pass through them easily; atherosclerosis furs them up with rough fibrous scabby deposits. And its effects are exactly what you would expect if a domestic water-pipe were furred up – the blood supply is impeded and the heart has to work harder to pump the blood around the body.

The exact mechanism by which atherosclerosis – these porridgey deposits – builds up on the insides of arteries is not completely understood, but it is apparent that choles-terol circulating in the bloodstream is a crucial ingredient in the process. Indeed, the atherosclerotic deposit itself largely consists of cholesterol, forming a fibrous bulge into the artery with a scabby top to it. This partially blocks off the artery, causing turbulence where there ought to be smooth uninterrupted blood flow. The atherosclerosis can cause a weakness in the artery that may eventually burst. In the worst cases the atherosclerotic area can block the artery completely; alternatively a bit of the scab that forms on top of the deposit can become detached and lodge across an artery elsewhere, again resulting in a blockage. If this occurs in the brain it can cause a stroke; in the eyes it can cause poor vision; it can cause kidney failure; and if the legs are affected it can cause pain, lameness and even gangrene.

It is the effect that the furring-up has on the coronary arteries – the arteries supplying the heart – that is most critical. This furring-up due to atherosclerosis takes place slowly, and it appears that the heart can cope with the early slight diminution in its supply of oxygen and nutrients. It can only cope up to a point however; beyond that point you will start to notice the symptoms of coronary heart disease.

- **Angina**. This is an intense, often vice-like gripping pain originating in the chest; in many sufferers it spreads up into the neck and even down the left arm; and it usually occurs during bouts of exercise, hard work or stress, when extra demands are made on the heart. It is due to the fact that the partially blocked coronary arteries cannot get enough blood and oxygen to the heart muscle to cope with these extra demands.
- If the blood supply to an area of the heart becomes restricted, that bit of heart muscle can start to deteriorate. A sudden extra burden placed on the heart – work, exercise, excitement – can then be too much for it and that bit of the heart muscle packs up, i.e. you have a **heart attack**. If the area involved is slight, the heart can function satisfactorily after a period of recovery, despite the fact that the heart attack has left it with a section of scar tissue.
- However, if the heart disease is too far advanced by the time the first heart attack strikes, the result is fatal – **sudden death**.

Cholesterol and heart disease

It is easy to state categorically that coronary heart disease is caused by atherosclerosis, a furring-up of the arteries. But what causes atherosclerosis? Unfortunately the answer is not nearly so clear-cut. There are a number of apparent causes, and probably many that we don't know about yet, and they all interrelate with one another so that there is no clear picture.

The one fact that does stand out is that the level of cholesterol in your bloodstream is the strongest predictor of your risk of heart disease, i.e. the higher the cholesterol level, the greater the risk of heart disease. This is not to say that if you have a high cholesterol level you will definitely go on to suffer from heart disease; there are so many other factors to take into account – whether you smoke, take exercise, have a family history of heart disease, for example – that we can only talk about the risk of heart disease, the likelihood of getting it.

What we can say is that for every 1 per cent increase in the blood cholesterol level there is a 2 per cent increased chance, in both men and women, of subsequently suffering from heart disease. Among men in the age group 30–49 the risk is even greater; one study showed a 10 per cent increase in the chance of heart disease for every 1 per cent increase in total blood cholesterol levels for these men.

Bearing out these figures, there are people who suffer from the inherited disorders FH (familial hypercholesterolaemia) and FCH (familial combined hyperlipidaemia) who are characterised by extremely high cholesterol levels in the blood. This gives them a much increased risk of heart disease; for example, men suffering from FH have an eightfold greater chance of suffering from coronary heart disease than unaffected men. Heart disease also tends to strike such individuals at a much younger age – often in the 20s and 30s in the case of men. And sadly, far from being rare disorders, FH and FCH are two of the most common inherited diseases we know of.

When you consider that over one-third of the weight of the atherosclerotic deposits that fur up the arteries consists of cholesterol, it is perhaps not surprising that cholesterol is such a high risk factor for heart disease. But it is not quite as simple as it seems. Without going into too many details, it is important to realise that the cholesterol that circulates in the bloodstream consists of a number of different types, of which low density lipoprotein and high density lipoprotein are the most important.

- **Low density lipoprotein** cholesterol **(LDL)** transports cholesterol from the liver to the rest of the body, including the deposits that fur-up the arteries.
- **High density lipoprotein** cholesterol **(HDL)** transports cholesterol from the body – and this includes the atherosclerotic deposits in the arteries – back to the liver, for eventual excretion.

From this it should be clear that LDL cholesterol is the principal predictor of risk of heart disease, as it is the LDL that helps to build up the atherosclerotic deposits that cause coronary heart disease. It is the baddy. In contrast, HDL cholesterol actually reduces the risk of coronary heart disease as it removes cholesterol from the atherosclerotic deposits in the arteries and transports it back to the liver so it can be broken down and excreted. It is therefore the goody in the plot.

There is a danger of getting bogged down by the mass of figures when trying to establish what are 'good' and 'bad' levels for blood cholesterol. Equally, it is easy to get obsessed by a single figure, ignoring other factors that influence the risk of onset of heart disease – lifestyle, family history, weight, blood pressure, for example. In general, though:

- The total blood cholesterol level should be down towards 5 mmol/l, or lower. If it is up towards 6.5 mmol/l you should get a more detailed breakdown of the figure, and should seek advice on diet and lifestyle. And if it is up towards 7.5 mmol/l, or above, you should definitely get a more detailed breakdown, and be seriously advised on diet and lifestyle.
- LDL cholesterol should be as low as possible, preferably under 5 mmol/l.
- HDL cholesterol should be as high as possible, preferably over 1 mmol/l.

The only other measurement that needs to concern us here is the level of another fat – triglyceride – in the bloodstream, as a high triglyceride level is also indicative of an increased risk of heart disease. Triglyceride levels tend to be raised by a high consumption of refined carbohydrates such as biscuits, pastries, white bread and, particularly, alcohol.

OTHER PROBLEMS

So far we have merely looked at the two principal results of eating a high-fat diet – being overweight and a high risk of heart disease. But there are many other problems that stem from this sort of diet, particularly if it is coupled with a sedentary lifestyle. For example, being overweight can lead to:

- Breathlessness and breathing difficulties.
- Bone and joint problems.
- Diabetes.
- High blood pressure.
- Gallstones.

In addition, the Cancer Education Co-ordinating Group of the United Kingdom and Republic of Ireland have detailed a ten-point code for lessening your risk of cancer, and it should come as no surprise to learn that three items on this list are:

- Avoid being overweight.
- Cut down on fatty foods.
- Eat plenty of fresh fruit and vegetables.

But perhaps the most important fact to take on board is that, by being implicated in all these problems – being overweight, breathlessness, high blood pressure, heart disease, even cancer – a high-fat diet generally tends to make you feel unfit and unhealthy. You may not be aware of this at the time, but if you switch over to a low-fat diet you will gradually find yourself feeling less lethargic, healthier and fitter.

4

THE LOW-FAT STRATEGY

So far in this book we have been describing problems –
eating too much, being overweight, even being obese, high
cholesterol levels, heart disease. In this chapter we want to
turn things round, and give you some solutions.

WHAT IS THE LOW-FAT STRATEGY?

There are three key features that you need to understand.

- You should eat **less fat**.
- You should eat the **right fats**.
- You should have plenty of **soluble fibre** in your diet.

Eat less fat

On page 21 we explained that the energy content of fat is
over twice as much as that of protein, and nearly three
times as much as that of carbohydrate. It follows that if
your meals are heavily loaded with fat then they will
contain a lot of energy, and if you don't take a lot of
exercise to burn up this energy you will inevitably put on
weight. A diet low in fat will therefore help to reduce the
number of kilocalories taken in, and thus aid weight
reduction.

It has been calculated that the average Western diet yields about 40–45 per cent of its energy from fat. This is not to say that 40 per cent of the diet by weight consists of fat, though. The important fact here is that fat contributes over twice as much energy, gram for gram, as carbohydrate and protein, so a smaller portion of fatty food will contribute more in the way of energy than a comparatively larger portion that is predominantly carbohydrate.

As a rough and ready guide, if 20 per cent of your diet by weight consists of fat, then 40 per cent of your energy supply will come from fat. And such a proportion is very easy to achieve when you remember that all the following foods have high proportions of fat:

- All fats and oils, including butter, margarine, lard, suet – even the 'healthier' margarines that are labelled 'high in polyunsaturates'.
- Visible fat on meat, streaky bacon, meat pies and pasties, sausages, pâtés, salamis, mince, sausagemeat.
- Whole milk, cream, cheese, whole-milk yoghurts, Greek yoghurt, whole-milk fromage frais.
- Deep-fat-fried foods, e.g. chips, crisps, foods cooked in batter and breadcrumbs.
- Biscuits, cakes, ice cream, pastries.

We are not suggesting that you cut out all these sorts of foods from your diet completely, merely that you reduce them and substitute low-fat or non-fat alternatives. This book is designed to show you that there are tasty and nutritious alternatives and all the recipes are designed around this simple premise.

Eat the right fats

The reduction of the total fat content of the diet is not the only aim. We also need to cut back on our intake of saturated fats – those fats that contain saturated fatty acids. All the evidence indicates that it is the amount of saturated fat we consume that has the most significant effect on our circulating cholesterol levels, and it is these blood cholesterol levels that are the strongest predictors of heart disease.

Saturated fats are largely animal derived. It follows that if you eat no animal products you immediately lower your chances of taking in saturated fats. Vegetarians sometimes consume low amounts of saturated fats, although if they eat a lot of dairy produce this is not the case; vegans, who eat no animal produce at all, stand a much better chance of reducing their saturated fat intake.

There are also some saturated fats of vegetable origin – coconut and coconut products, for example, and palm oil. In addition, and more significantly, the processing of vegetable oils in the food industry also results in the production of saturated fats. The key phrase to look out for and avoid is 'hydrogenated vegetable oil'; this means that the polyunsaturated vegetable oils have had hydrogen incorporated into their molecular structure so that they become saturated – hydrogenated in this case means saturated.

As well as reducing the proportion of saturated fat in our dietary fat intake, there is also strong evidence that we should increase the proportion of mono-unsaturated fat. This is not to say that we should consume masses of mono-unsaturated fats; we should still aim for a low-fat diet, but the limited amount of fat that we do consume should predominantly be mono-unsaturated. The basis for this advice is that mono-unsaturated fats have been shown to raise the levels of HDL cholesterol in the blood, and you will remember that HDL cholesterol is the 'goody', as it actually reduces the deposits that fur up the arteries and cause heart disease. This certainly seems to be the case with people who live in traditional Mediterranean areas and whose diets are particularly rich in mono-unsaturated fats.

But where can you get mono-unsaturated fats? The richest source of MUFAs is olive oil, and you may have already noticed the promotion of olive oil as a healthy cooking oil, the low incidence of coronary heart disease in the Mediterranean areas (where they use lots of olive oil)

31

being quoted as evidence for this supposition. The problem is that olive oil is expensive. Furthermore it has a very distinctive taste, which is fine in salads and savoury dishes but may be out of place in other recipes.

Three other oils that are readily available and that are rich in MUFAs are peanut or groundnut oil, rapeseed oil and grapeseed oil. They are not nearly as expensive as olive oil, and they certainly don't have such a distinctive taste.

But what about the polyunsaturated fats that everyone talks about? Should we forget about them completely? The answer to this last question is definitely no. Polyunsaturated fats provide important constituents of the diet – some of the polyunsaturated fatty acids are in fact essential. The advice is therefore to reduce your overall intake of fat, to try and ensure that mono-unsaturated fats constitute the largest proportion of this reduced content, with polyunsaturated fats taking up the next largest share.

Lastly we come to the place of cholesterol in the diet. There is debate within the medical world as to how much the intake of cholesterol in the diet affects blood cholesterol levels. Certainly dietary cholesterol doesn't affect blood cholesterol levels nearly as much as saturated fat intake does. However, if we want to lower blood cholesterol levels we do need to keep an eye on dietary cholesterol intake, for the simple reason that dietary cholesterol is usually found in foods that also contain significant proportions of saturated fats, e.g.:

- Eggs, the yolks containing all the cholesterol.
- Offal such as liver, kidney, heart.
- Butter and many hard cheeses such as Cheddar and Stilton.

Seafoods such as crab, lobster and shrimps contain significant proportions of cholesterol, but they also have high proportions of polyunsaturated fats, so should not figure on any 'banned' list – although given their price they're not the sort of foods you're likely to be eating every day.

32

And because of their relatively high fat content they should certainly be limited items in a low-fat diet.

To summarise, the advice on fats is straightforward.

- **Reduce the fat intake**. It should comprise no more than 30–35 per cent of the energy content of the diet, which translates as 15 per cent of the intake by weight, or less. This is the most important piece of advice.
- **Mono-unsaturates should make up the largest proportion** of the fats consumed; aim for mono-unsaturates comprising half the total of fats, if possible.
- **Polyunsaturates should make up the next largest proportion** of fats consumed.
- **Saturated fats should make up the smallest proportion** of fats; reducing the consumption of saturated fats is the other important piece of advice.
- Aim to keep the cholesterol intake low.

FIBRE

If you are going to cut down your fat intake, what are you going to replace it with? The simple answer is fibre, which is found in fruit, vegetables and cereals. For example, four to five portions of high fibre foods a day are easily achieved if you have cereal for breakfast, potato and a second vegetable with your main meal, some fruit or salad with another meal, and perhaps a piece of fruit as a snack at some other time during the day. But remember, full-fat milk on your cereal or cream on your fruit add to the intake of saturated fat, as do most sauces, custards and similar accompaniments.

The overall aim in increasing your intake of carbohydrates, particularly the high fibre type, is to provide over half of your energy needs. Meals based on this premise will be substantial, because of the bulk associated with the filling complex carbohydrates. Furthermore, because such

33

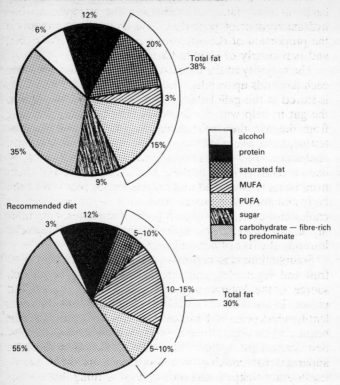

Usual diet in most Western industrialised countries

12%

6%

20%

Total fat
38%

3%

35%

15%

9%

alcohol
protein
saturated fat
MUFA
PUFA
sugar
carbohydrate — fibre-rich
to predominate

Recommended diet

12%

3%

5–10%

10–15%

Total fat
30%

55%

5–10%

The proportions of the diet, by energy content (not weight), in a typical Western country and in the recommended low-fat cholesterol lowering diet

carbohydrate takes time to digest, the bloodstream does not receive sudden surges of simple sugars like glucose; instead the products of digestion appear in the bloodstream over a period of time – it is a sort of slow-release system.

But there is a further significant advantage to cutting back on your fats and increasing the complex carbohydrate content of your diet. You automatically increase the proportion of the different types of fibre in your diet, and particularly of soluble fibre.

The majority of the cholesterol that our bodies produce each day ends up as bile – the bile is produced in the liver, is stored in the gallbladder, from where it is released into the gut to help with fat digestion. The bile salts resulting from the bile then pass down the gut into the large intestine, from where they are re-absorbed and recycled into cholesterol. But if there is any soluble fibre in the food mass it tends to cling to these bile salts and prevent them from being re-absorbed and recycled; they pass out of the body and are thus removed from what might be called the cholesterol cycle. The overall level of cholesterol circulating in the bloodstream is in this way reduced, thereby lowering the risk of heart disease.

Soluble fibre is found, to a greater or lesser extent, in all fruit and vegetables, and cereals such as oats, but a rich source is the legume vegetables – the peas, beans and pulses. In particular, the dried pulses such as split peas, lentils, chickpeas, red kidney beans, soya beans, haricot beans and so on, and including baked beans, are all very rich sources of soluble fibre. From this it should be apparent that cooking with foods such as dried beans, lentils and chickpeas can only be a good thing if you want to reduce your risk of heart disease:

- They are a good source of protein, so can be substituted for meat, thus reducing the intake of saturated fat.
- They are a good source of complex carbohydrate.
- They are a good source of soluble fibre – the soluble complex carbohydrate – which removes bile salts from the 'cholesterol cycle'.

Another very good source of soluble fibre is oats, and it is recommended that oats and oatmeal be incorporated into the diet where it is reasonable – they are both tasty thickeners and binding agents. Oat bran is the part of the oat grain that is richest in soluble fibre; it can be used as an addition to many recipes, is found in many of the newer breakfast cereals, and will certainly help in the effect soluble fibre has on cholesterol levels.

The important point is to remember that we are talking about soluble fibre. Insoluble fibre – ordinary wheat bran, for example – certainly helps digestion in general, but it is inert, merely adding bulk to the food mass in the digestive tract. Soluble fibre from fruit and vegetables, peas and bean, oats, oat bran and some other cereals, dissolves in water and other substances and can play an active role in affecting, among other things, blood cholesterol levels and thus the risk of heart disease.

THE RESULTS

So, what should be the result of this low-fat diet that we are proposing?

- To begin with, you should gradually **lose weight**.
- Unlike most diets, we are not suggesting you should eat less food, merely that you should eat less fat; because of this you should have **no hunger pangs**.
- This diet should at the same time **lower your risk of heart disease**.

Weight loss

You will remember that a typical Western diet consists of 20 per cent by weight of fat, equivalent to 40 per cent energy intake from fat. If instead you were able to reduce the fat content of your diet to 15 per cent by weight or less, there would be two immediate consequences:

- You would immediately reduce the energy supplied by fat to about 30–35 per cent or less of the total energy intake from your food.

- You would also probably reduce your overall energy intake, as you would be hard put to eat enough carbohydrate to keep the energy supply up to the previous total – for every gram of fat not eaten you would have to eat nearly 3 grams of carbohydrate or over 2 grams of protein to supply the same amount of energy.

Therefore if you reduced your total fat intake you would probably reduce your total energy intake, which in turn would mean that you would probably lose weight; you'd certainly stand much less chance of gaining weight.

What tends to happen when you switch over to a low-fat diet is that you do indeed tend to lose weight, sometimes spectacularly but usually slowly and steadily. You may even dip down below what might be considered your comfortable weight, but as your body adjusts to your dietary changes you will gradually settle at what might be called your natural weight.

No hunger pangs

What is also important to realise is that this reduction in weight can be achieved without any reduction in the quantity of food you consume, merely a change in emphasis.

This is unlike the majority of diets, where you are advised to cut down on the overall intake of food. These invariably require a lot of willpower to adhere to, and can leave you at the end of one meal already anticipating the next, with the hunger pangs gradually increasing over the hours. Because of this, the diet comes to dominate your life, with all sorts of feelings of guilt if you break out of it to satisfy the hunger pangs.

With the low-fat diet, if you feel hungry between meals you can go and eat anything you like, as long as it has little or no fat in it. If you have hunger pangs, by all means assuage them, but with a piece of fruit or a fat-free biscuit, not with a bacon butty or a chocolate biscuit.

Less risk of heart disease

The loss in weight is a visible benefit from this diet; the lower risk of heart disease that it also brings is much less visible but arguably much more important. In particular, this low-fat diet will be of great help to those people suffering from the inherited disorders of cholesterol metabolism known as FH and FCH (see page 26) – disorders characterised by extremely high blood cholesterol levels.

The decrease in the risk of heart disease flows from three features of the diet:

- There is a reduction in the intake of saturated fat. As saturated fat intake has the greatest influence on the level of cholesterol in the bloodstream, and the cholesterol level is in turn the greatest risk factor for heart disease, any reduction in the saturated fat intake is going to have a direct impact on the risk of heart disease.
- There is an increase in the proportion of mono-unsaturated fats in the diet. MUFAs tend to raise the level of HDL cholesterol in the blood, and this in turn can help reverse the build up of cholesterol-rich deposits in the blood vessels, thus lowering the risk of heart disease.
- The high proportion of complex carbohydrates in the diet ensure you obtain plenty of soluble fibre. Soluble fibre removes the bile salts from the digestive tract, and this in turn lowers the level of cholesterol in the bloodstream, again lowering the risk of heart disease.

These factors have all been discussed already in this book. But there is one other feature of the diet that needs stressing here. On a low-fat diet you will tend to stabilise at your natural weight, often losing weight in the process. We have mentioned that there are a number of risk factors for heart disease, of which having a high cholesterol level is one of the most critical. Another risk factor, albeit of lesser importance, is being overweight; various studies have shown that there is a direct increase in risk of coronary heart disease with increase in weight above your ideal weight. By bringing you down to this ideal weight, the low-fat diet tends to reduce yet another of the risk factors for heart disease.

A HEALTHIER LIFE

So far in this chapter we have looked at what the low-fat diet involves, and the benefits it brings – indeed this is the primary aim of the book. But if you want to lose weight and reduce your risks of heart disease, you can't merely change your diet while ignoring other aspects of your life.

Smoking

Unfortunately we're stuck with cigarettes, and with all the health risks they bring with them. Note that we don't say we *think* there are health risks; we *know* very definitely there are health risks. The links between smoking and lung cancer have been well documented. But there are also very well-documented and proven links between smoking and the risk of coronary heart disease; people who smoke more than 20 cigarettes a day have about double the risk of coronary heart disease as non-smokers, and it takes about a year of non-smoking for a reformed smoker's risk to drop to that of a permanent non-smoker of similar age. In fact, smoking is far more of a risk than being over-weight, so it is unfortunate that putting on weight can be a side effect of giving up smoking, as it can deter many people who might wish to stop the habit.

The advice is therefore to stop smoking, for a multitude of reasons, and this advice applies in particular to women. Women are in some way protected against the risks of coronary heart disease by high levels of the female sex hormones circulating in their bloodstream before the menopause; after the menopause these hormones diminish, as does the protection against heart disease. But smoking somehow seems to bring on the age of menopause earlier, so not only does smoking add its own risks as regards heart disease, but for women it also appears to remove their natural protection against risk at an earlier age.

Exercise

There are many reasons for taking exercise, ignoring the benefits of feeling in better health generally. For a start, if you take more exercise, you use up more of the energy that you take in your food, thus reducing your chances of putting on weight.

Furthermore, it makes your heart stronger. If you take exercise your heart has to pump more blood round the body to service the muscles you're using; if you take regular exercise the heart acclimatises to this new regime and gets bigger and stronger, so that it can work more efficiently. As a result of this and other factors, any tendency to raised blood pressure is also reduced.

But exercise also seems to have a direct effect on the blood cholesterol level:

- Regular exercise **lowers the LDL cholesterol levels**, and you will remember that the LDL level is the strongest predictor of risk of heart disease.
- Regular brisk exercise **raises the HDL cholesterol levels**, and this in turn further reduces the risk of heart disease.

While not wishing to discourage people, what is meant here is not a gentle amble round the park with the dog; this is fine in its way, and is certainly better than nothing. Brisk exercise means, for example, a mile or two's walk with one stiffish hill. The aim is to raise your pulse rate by a significant amount. However, care must be taken to increase the level gradually.

Alcohol

Note that this section is not headed 'Reduce your alcohol level' or 'Stop drinking'. Alcohol in itself is not a problem;

indeed some studies have shown that a daily glass or two (and no more) of wine, or the equivalent, might be instrumental in raising the HDL cholesterol level, which is protective against heart disease.

Excessive alcohol consumption, however, is a problem. It can undermine people's lives and their families' lives, it can have a profound effect on health, it can result in gross obesity, and it can be a risk factor for heart disease. In previous chapters we have seen how alcohol consumption can have an impact on the triglyceride levels in the bloodstream, and it has been explained that high blood triglyceride levels are a risk factor in their own right for heart disease.

You may feel that there is no way that you could be a heavy drinker. This is probably true; but try keeping a diary of alcohol consumption, and you might be surprised at how much you get through in a week, especially when you consider what the recommended maximum weekly consumption is:

- For a man the guideline is 21 units per week, equivalent to 21 glasses of wine or $10^{1}/_{2}$ pints of beer.
- For a woman it is 14 units per week, i.e. 14 glasses of wine or 7 pints of beer.

If you are slightly over this limit there is no great cause for concern, although you would be advised to consider cutting back on one or two drinks. However, if your weekly total is two or three times this limit you would be advised to speak to your GP about it.

5

THE HEALTHY KITCHEN

Later on in the book you will find all the recipes you'll need to get you started on a low-fat diet. In this chapter, by way of an introduction, we will take you through some of the important ingredients you'll be working with, some of the cooking techniques you'll need to know about, and the equipment you'll want.

INGREDIENTS

In this section we will guide you through the basic ingredients that are used in any kitchen and show you how they can be fitted in to a low-fat diet.

Cooking oils and fats

If you have already read the previous chapters you will have grasped the fact that in a low-fat diet:

- We need to reduce the overall amount of fat in the diet.
- Within that reduced amount of fat, the mono-unsaturated fats should constitute the largest proportion, followed by the polyunsaturates. This is

important from the point of view of lowering your risk of heart disease.

The first point is well known, and many people nowadays would accept it as common sense. The second point is a fairly recent piece of dietary advice; until now it has been thought that it was merely important to lower the proportion of saturated fats and raise the proportion of polyunsaturates and mono-unsaturates together. Consequently manufacturers have concentrated on producing, and publicising, oils and spreads high in polyunsaturates, and have largely forgotten about the mono-unsaturates.

Classification of fats and oils

Saturated	Mono-unsaturated	Polyunsaturated
Palm kernel oil	Olive oil	Sunflower oil
Coconut oil	Peanut (groundnut) oil	Safflower oil
Butter	Rapeseed oil	Corn oil
Lard	Grapeseed oil	Soya oil
Hard margarine		Walnut oil
Suet		Margarines and
Vegetarian suet		spreads labelled
Standard soft		high in polyun-
margarine		saturates

The accompanying table lists the commonly available oils and fats, and indicates which category they fall into, although it ought to be borne in mind that these are not strict delimitations; for example, although peanut (groundnut) oil is listed as a mono-unsaturate, it also contains about 30 per cent polyunsaturated fats and 20 per cent saturated fats.

What you need to be doing, therefore, is to:

- Cut out all the fats and oils on the list of saturates.

43

- Use mono-unsaturated oils in your cooking, salad dressings and so on whenever it is feasible. This does not mean use mono-unsaturated oils whenever possible; merely, when a cooking oil is needed use a small amount of mono-unsaturated oil.
- When a hard fat or spread is needed, use one that is high in polyunsaturated fat, but keep an eye out for similar products that might appear on the market labelled high in mono-unsaturates.

You may feel that it is next to impossible to substitute a mono-unsaturated oil such as rapeseed oil in all the recipes that ordinarily ask you to use hard margarine or butter. However, it is not as difficult as you might think; in many recipes, such as pastry, crumble topping, biscuits and cakes, you can substitute a mono-unsaturated oil such as rapeseed or peanut oil, as long as you remember the magic conversion factor:

- 5 tbsp (75 ml) of oil are equivalent to 4 oz (100 grams) of hard margarine or butter.

Milk and other dairy produce
The fat content of ordinary milk is not high – 3.7 grams of fat per 100 grams of milk – but because milk is consumed in relatively large quantities you should be aware of the total amount of fat you are consuming. For example, if you have a pint of milk (600 ml) during the course of a day, that will add about 20 grams of fat to your intake. Single cream has a higher fat content, double cream is even higher, and clotted cream is in a class of its own.

For these reasons it is sensible to use skimmed milk and semi-skimmed milk instead of whole milk. All contain similar amounts of protein, vitamins and minerals.

- Skimmed milk has had virtually all the fat content removed.
- Semi-skimmed milk still has some fat content, but considerably less than whole milk.

44

Many people find skimmed milk too thin and unpalatable for everyday use, for example on their breakfast cereal or in their tea. Nevertheless it is worth trying, perhaps after acclimatising the taste buds to semi-skimmed milk for a few weeks. In cooking, though, skimmed milk can be used with impunity. You might arrive at a compromise, in which semi-skimmed milk is used for tea, cereals and so on and skimmed milk is used in cooking.

But what about recipes that call for the use of cream? Or puddings that cry out for a blob of cream on top? It is possible to buy low-fat cream nowadays, but an alternative, particularly for toppings, is to make use of the plain, virtually fat-free yoghurts and fromage frais; these are not a substitute for cream, merely an alternative, but their advantage is that virtually fat-free means just that – a fat content as low as less than 0.1 gram per 100 grams.

Goats' and sheep's milk are not a sensible option if you are aiming for a low-fat diet, as both have higher fat contents than cows' milk; goats' milk is significantly higher, at 4.8 grams of fat for every 100 grams of milk, and sheep's milk is nearly twice as fatty, with 6.9 grams of fat per 100 grams of milk. Both of these milks, and cheeses, yoghurts, etc., made from them, should therefore be avoided.

Cheese

If you are adopting a low-fat diet, one fact that you might find hard to face up to is that cheese is essentially a high-fat food. Cheese (and chocolate) has such a strong taste that it often becomes almost an addiction with some people, and asking them to cut down on or remove cheese from their diet is a tall order.

For a start you need to realise that some cheeses have a higher fat content than others. The labels on the cheeses are not necessarily much help in this respect; in Europe they tend to give the fat content as a proportion of the dry weight of the cheese, i.e. minus any water content the cheese might have, while in the UK the fat content is given as a proportion of the wet weight of the cheese. A French

Cheese	Fat content (g per 100 g dry weight)
St Paulin, Edam, Gouda	23
Brie, Camembert	23
Roquefort, Danish Blue	29
Cheddar, Gruyère, Emmenthal	34
Stilton	40
Cream cheese	47
Cottage cheese	0.4

Camembert cheese labelled 45 per cent fat content (45 per cent *matière graisse*) is only about 23 per cent fat content using the UK wet weight calculation. The accompanying table gives the fat contents of a selection of cheeses.

Manufacturers are now producing low-fat hard cheeses, such as a Cheddar type, with as little as 14 per cent fat content, but using such a cheese in any quantity in a recipe still bumps up the fat content of each serving quite considerably. The broad advice is therefore to try and avoid cooking with cheese.

There are various soft cheeses produced nowadays with very low-fat contents – low-fat curd cheese or cottage cheese, for example. These make good sandwich fillings, especially when mixed with other ingredients, or can be incorporated into flan fillings, for example, without producing a high fat content.

Eggs

The first thing to say about eggs is that the medical world is divided about the impact they make on circulating cholesterol levels and thus on the risk of heart disease; some studies show a significant impact, other studies show the opposite. The advice we give here is therefore a compromise, and is as follows: If you are adopting a low-fat diet you should consume no more than two to three whole eggs per week.

It is easy to limit the consumption of eggs on their own – boiled eggs, scrambled eggs and so on – but how are you going to cook without eggs? How do you make cakes without eggs, for example, or flans? At first sight it might appear that the cooking is going to be a little dull.

- The first thing to realise is that it is the egg yolk that is rich in cholesterol and saturated fats – the egg white has no cholesterol, is rich in protein, and sets when heated. So one option is to use eggs, but throw the yolks away. This is, however, extremely wasteful, so you may want to consider other options.
- Many dishes that you thought had to include eggs can be made without them; we have given flan and cake recipes without eggs in later chapters.
- There are a number of egg replacers on the market that are based on egg white alone; these can be used in many recipes instead of eggs.

Meat

A low-fat diet does not mean that you have to become a vegetarian or a vegan. While it might be advisable to reduce your use of meat and consume more vegetables, if you choose your meat carefully you can lower the fat content of your meals dramatically.

To begin with, although it might seem obvious to state this, buy meat that has little visible fat on it. For example, avoid streaky bacon; instead get back bacon, and cut the fat off before cooking it. Ask for lean cuts of beef, lamb and pork, and trim off any remaining fat before you use it. Remember that chicken and turkey meat are low in fat, although the skin is high in fat and should be removed. In contrast, most meat products, such as sausages, meat pâtés, salamis, luncheon meats, pies and pasties are very high in fat.

Two types of meat that tend to be low in fat are organic meat and game, e.g. rabbit, pheasant, pigeon and venison. Of the two, the organically farmed meat tends to be fattier, but the fat content in both meats has a much lower proportion of saturated fats, and a correspondingly higher proportion of polyunsaturates and mono-unsaturates, than the intensively farmed meat you usually find on the shelves of your supermarket or at your butchers. You will undoubtedly find these meats more expensive than intensively farmed meat, but they are much stronger in flavour so you tend not to consume such large quantities.

Fish

In contrast to meat, fish – even the oily fish – have a much lower fat content, and what fat they do have is poly-unsaturated. In particular, they tend to contain a group of polyunsaturates that make the blood less sticky, and because of this are very good at reducing the risk of heart disease; from the point of view of heart disease, the advice is to include fish in the diet at least a couple of times a week. Shellfish are to be recommended as they tend to contain the lowest levels of fat, and recipes usually only specify a small amount of shellfish per serving.

Furthermore, fish are also an excellent source of the fat-soluble vitamin D. Vitamin D can be made in the body by the action of sunlight on the skin, and can be obtained from dairy products. However, on a low-fat diet you may not be eating enough dairy produce to guarantee a high enough intake of this vitamin. Eating plenty of fish is therefore a very healthy way of ensuring an adequate level of vitamin D.

What is not advised, though, is to fry the fish. Frying, and especially deep-fat frying, immediately bumps up the fat content of a fish dish, usually with saturated fats. And fish and chips has an extremely high fat content associated with it as a result of deep-fat frying both the fish and the potatoes.

Flour

Flour is obviously an essential part of your store-cupboard, and contains only negligible quantities of fat – typically, 1 gram per 100 grams. The advice here is merely to try and use wholemeal flour wherever possible; it has a much higher content of dietary fibre than processed flour, and is a complex carbohydrate, processed flour being more in the way of a simple carbohydrate.

Oats

As we have explained earlier, oats are a rich source of soluble fibre, which has a particular beneficial impact on the risk of heart disease, as well as being a very good source of complex carbohydrates. However, they are also a very versatile cereal, whether used as oatmeal, oat bran flakes or whole oats; oats can be used as a coating, e.g. for grilled fish, as a topping, as a thickening agent, as a binding agent, and in many instances can be used as a substitute for wheat flour – for example, on page 172 there is a recipe for rolled oats pastry.

Other cereals

Do not think that the cereals in your store-cupboard should be limited to wheat flour, with the occasional use of oats. A wide range of cereals are available now which can be incorporated, to a greater or lesser extent, in your cooking.

The obvious one, perhaps, is rice. Rice is very nutritious, has a minimal fat content and is rich in soluble fibre, particularly the wholegrain varieties. It can be incorporated in both hot and cold meals. But what about millet and couscous? They can both be used in many recipes instead of rice, either as a base for hot meals or stirred into salads. Barley and rye flakes can both be used in homemade muesli (see page 62).

Beans and pulses

Dried beans and pulses – lentils, red beans, chickpeas, butter beans, soya beans and so on – should be an important ingredient in any low-fat diet.

- They are rich sources of low biological value proteins (see page 8).

- They are very low in fat – typically 1.5 gram per 100 grams.
- Their carbohydrate content is high, and is complex carbohydrate.
- They are tasty, the coloured varieties – red beans, green mung beans, black beans, black eye beans – look attractive, and they are very cheap.

Before dried beans can be used they need soaking overnight, and without a pressure cooker they can take quite a time to cook, which you might see as a disadvantage. If so, various canned precooked beans and pulses are widely available as an alternative, although these are more expensive, and are often packed in salt/sugar water, so rinse them thoroughly before use.

Fruit and vegetables

If you are cutting down the fat content of your diet your aim should be to increase the complex carbohydrate content to make up the difference in quantity. And, while cereals, beans and pulses are valuable sources of complex carbohydrate, and should be important features of your diet, it cannot be emphasised enough that you should eat plenty of fruit and vegetables, both raw and cooked (but not overcooked).

It should be obvious by now that fruit and vegetables are extremely low in fat, with a few exceptions such as avocados and nuts, and are rich in complex carbohydrates. Just as importantly, they are rich in vitamins and other valuable nutrients, they invariably contain a high proportion of soluble fibre, and they are low in calories while at the same time they fill you up.

The aim should be to have four to five portions of fruit and vegetables each day. This might sound a lot, but is not difficult to achieve; for example, potato and one or two vegetables with your main meal, some fruit and/or salad with another meal, and perhaps a piece of fruit as a snack at some other time of day.

A few tips to bear in mind are:

- Use fresh fruit and vegetables wherever possible, not tinned, dried or frozen varieties; fresh produce always tastes much better, and is richer in essential nutrients such as vitamins.

- Throw as little of the fruit or vegetables away. Potato skins contain a high proportion of the fibre, nutrients and taste, as do carrot skins – scrub them, don't peel them.

- When cooking vegetables and fruit do not overcook them. Apart from the fact that you lose a lot of flavour, you also lose a lot of nutrients such as vitamins. In most cases cooked vegetables and fruit should have some crispness or bite to them.

- If you can afford it, buy organic fruit and vegetables. Not only are they free from chemicals, but they invariably have a much stronger taste than the intensively grown equivalent. Or grow your own.

Seasonings

It should be obvious that none of the customary seasonings are likely to contribute to our overall fat intake. However, there are other factors to consider.

To begin with, it is generally considered that we consume too much sodium – particularly from salt – and that this can lead to a number of health problems. The most serious of these problems is the link between salt and high blood pressure (hypertension), which in turn carries a significant risk of heart disease. If you or anyone else in your family is prone to high blood pressure, then you will need to adapt your diet accordingly – you will need to cut down not only on the salt intake, but also limit the amount of sodium you get, for example from convenience foods, packet foods, canned soups, cheeses, cured meats and salted nuts.

In general we tend to rely far too much on salt and other salt-based seasonings such as garlic salt and celery salt. We automatically tip salt into cooking water, into rice dishes, into stews, casseroles, curries and sauces. At table we make lavish use of salt, sprinkling it over every savoury dish as a matter of course, without ever thinking to check whether or not it needs it. Try cutting back on the amount you use in your cooking; try tasting a dish first, to see if it really does need extra salt, before you attack it with the salt cellar.

Monosodium glutamate is another rich source of sodium in our typical Western diet – it crops up in stock cubes, Bovril, Marmite, soy sauce and many convenience and packet foods. Try to avoid these products, or use them sparingly. Stock cubes, for example, can often be dispensed with by preparing your own stock or by using the water you cook vegetables in.

You should also realise that there are alternatives to salt.

- There are low sodium salts such as Lo-Salt that have a similar taste to the real thing but as little as one-third the sodium content.
- Or try to make more use of pepper instead. Black pepper has a much more distinctive flavour than white pepper, which is simply hot. If possible, use freshly milled black pepper, i.e. peppercorns in a pepper mill, both for cooking and at the table.
- Make wider use of herbs and spices, always trying to obtain fresh herbs and freshly ground spices; for example, it is just as easy to grate some nutmeg yourself as it is to use a pot of ground nutmeg you bought years ago. Use freshly chopped ginger instead of some tired old ground ginger powder.
- Get used to using fruit juices (lemon juice, for example, or other unsweetened juices), essences, mustards and vinegars (a very wide range is available now). But avoid the processed flavourings that list salt as a principal ingredient.

COOKING TECHNIQUES AND EQUIPMENT

In this section we summarise the various cooking techniques, their advantages from the point of view of a low-fat diet, and the equipment that is involved with each technique.

Raw food

In Western cooking only fruits and vegetables are served raw, the exceptions being oysters and steak tartare. However, in Japanese cooking extremely fresh fish and parts of the chicken breast are served raw, while in Indonesia (and Holland) there are also dishes based on raw fish. In such dishes the appeal is as much aesthetic as gastronomic – there is a purity of flavour, and the quality of the food is not interfered with. Furthermore, the vitamin and nutrient content of raw food is higher than cooked food.

When we think of raw food, though, invariably we think of salads. Any green leaves used in a salad – lettuces of various kinds, chicory, radicchio, sorrel, watercress, young spinach – must not only be washed but also dried thoroughly, otherwise any dressing will not adhere. A salad spinner is very useful for this purpose; alternatively pat the leaves dry using a clean tea towel.

To prepare fruit and vegetables you will need top quality knives and a solid chopping board. Traditionally, hardwood boards, solid and seamless, have been chosen for chopping, but there is now a heavy emphasis on hygiene, and many people are turning to white polyethylene synthetic blocks. These new blocks do not blunt the knives, although they do score like wood; their advantage is that they can be easily washed in very hot water.

The best knives are made of plain – rustable – carbon steel, and can be sharpened easily on a butcher's steel. You will need a minimum of three:

- One large knife for cutting meat, fish and large and solid vegetables.
- A medium-sized one for general purpose work.
- And a small one for vegetables, fruit and fine work.

A vegetable peeler is an almost essential addition.

Such knives should be washed by hand, dried immediately and stored in a block or on a magnetic rack. This is much safer than keeping them loose in a drawer, and means the edges don't get blunted or damaged by knocking against each other.

When preparing vegetables for serving raw, try and serve them whole if possible, e.g. mushrooms, or break them into pieces, e.g. the florets of cauliflower and calabrese. Otherwise cut them into uniformly sized pieces as far as possible. There will be a need to prepare vegetables in smaller pieces for some dishes, though, and a good stainless steel grater is very useful from this point of view. A processor can be used for chopping, slicing and grating, although the end result can sometimes be a bit too fine.

Frying

Contrary to many people's ideas, it is possible to deep-fat fry food when on a low-fat diet. If food is fried properly the fat does not enter it, the temperature being high enough to form a crisp outer coating. At lower temperatures, though, the fat does get into the food and makes it soggy; similarly, if you put too much into the fat at one go the temperature drops and the same thing happens. However, if the temperature is too high the outside of the food will be burned before the inside is cooked. It's a question of using a good oil (groundnut/peanut is one of the best), and if possible not trying to cook too much or too large pieces in one go.

Having said that, on a low-fat diet you are more commonly going to be sauté-ing food, i.e. cooking food in a frying pan with the minimum of oil needed to stop the pieces of food sticking together. The food is then tossed while it is cooking (*sauter* being the French for 'to jump'). As with other cooking techniques, good pans are essential; they should be heavy-bottomed so they don't tip over easily and so that they ensure an even distribution of the heat.

Stir-frying is becoming increasingly popular nowadays,

the essential piece of equipment here being a wok. Modern woks are made from thin carbon steel, and have a slightly flattened bottom so that they can sit on a hob. Unfortunately, woks are less well suited to electric hobs than to the all-round easily adjusted heat of a gas flame.

Speed is of the essence in stir-frying. The vegetables, meat or fish to be cooked should be cut, sliced or diced to the same size, and should be added to the hot oil in the order that ensures that they will all be ready at the same time. It helps if all the separate ingredients are ready to hand in separate bowls or saucers, and can then be added without having to interrupt the cooking. Use a spatula to keep the food constantly moving.

Steaming

This is a very pure form of cooking much used in Japan, China and other Oriental countries, and is unquestionably the best way of cooking fish, particularly white fish, and green vegetables. It is not a particularly fast way of cooking, especially if the boiling water has to be topped up, but can be speeded up by using smaller pieces of food.

Fold-up steamers that fit into saucepans are fiddly (and therefore dangerous) and too small to be very versatile. Bamboo steamers are good-looking, cheap and efficient, and can easily be placed over a saucepan or wok of boiling liquid. All-in-one aluminium or stainless steel steamers are much more expensive, but are worth it if you are converted to steaming. The best ones have two or three tiers so that you can cook a number of different items at once.

Grilling

For grilling you can use a gas flame, an electric grill or a charcoal barbecue – all provide a dry intense radiant heat that cooks food very rapidly. Because of the dry heat grilling is therefore unsuitable for tough cuts of meat and for dryish fish such as halibut, but is ideal for oily fish such as mackerel – slash the skin if necessary to stop them curling up. It is also very useful for foods such as steak

55

that do not have to be cooked right the way through; if you do want to cook something right through, move the grill rack further away from the heat or wait until the charcoal has died down a bit, and take longer over the cooking. Whatever you're cooking, though, it will need to be constantly watched; too long on the grill rack – especially white fish – and you've had it.

On a low-fat diet, grilling is particularly useful when cooking meat, as any fat in the meat is inclined to run out. However, in order to retain a pleasant moist texture and flavour, marinating is often advisable. Marinades include an ingredient to tenderise the food – wine, vinegar or yoghurt – and others to add flavour, such as herbs, spices, garlic and onion. Some meats will also need a little oil in the marinade; this will soak in and keep the meat soft during cooking. Foods not marinated will probably need basting throughout grilling.

When turning the grilled food use tongs rather than a fork, as a fork will pierce the surface and let juices and flavour run out.

Roasting

Strictly speaking roasting should be the latter-day equivalent of the open-fire technique of cooking on a spit, in which someone was always at hand to baste the meat. For meats to be roasted successfully they must retain their moisture and flavour, and this is best achieved by sprinkling a trace of flour over the meat before cooking. Do not insert a fork or a skewer into the meat during cooking, and never baste it – basting merely washes all the juices and flavour away. And there is absolutely no need to have a piece of meat roasting in a pool of fat; instead place the meat on a rack in the roasting tray so that all the fat that runs out can collect under the joint, not around it.

A metal baking tin with a wire rack in it is ideal for roasting. When the meat is cooked it should stand for a minimum of 15 minutes, and during this time the gravy can be prepared. Drain off any fat remaining in the baking tin, pour in some of the cooking water from the vegetables, and/or some wine if you want, simmer on the hob and scrape up the cooking residues from the meat, transfer to a small saucepan and reduce until it thickens. Alternatively use a little flour to thicken the gravy.

Baking

The semi-dry heat of an oven is ideal not only for pastries, cakes and bread mixtures, but also for fish, either in pieces or wrapped up in greaseproof paper parcels or envelopes – *en papillote*. Or the fish can be placed on a bed of vegetables and herbs and covered with aluminium foil. A pie covered with mashed potato is also a form of baking.

Pot-roasting or braising

This is a form of cooking in which a pot is covered with a lid, perhaps with the further addition of a flour-and-water pastry to seal the lid, and the contents are cooked slowly in their own juices and flavours. This is ideal for tougher cuts of meat and larger chickens, for example, to which no extra fat needs to be added.

An earthenware pot is best for this type of cooking.

Stewing

This is best in a cast iron or enamelled casserole as the process is carried out on top of the stove, simmering the contents slowly to keep them on the move in the cooking liquid. It is also a very good technique for tough cuts of meat, but they should be cut into small pieces first and fried in the minimum of oil in order to seal the pieces.

You can skim off any fat that rises to the surface during the cooking. Alternatively, and preferably, you can cook the meal a day in advance, allowing the fat to set and making it much easier to remove with a spatula.

Boiling and poaching

For boiling food you will need a range of saucepans, and preferably pans with heavy bottoms. And you should always remember that very few foods need to be cooked in fiercely boiling water – even pasta and rice, which should certainly go into water that is boiling fast, should actually be cooked at a more moderate pace.

Fresh vegetables should be cooked in as little water as possible until they are just done, thus preserving nutritional content, colour and 'bite'. The cooking water can then be saved for stock or soups, so that none of the nutrients are thrown away.

Meat and fish should certainly not be boiled too fast or for too long, unless of course you specifically want the stock. If the fish or meat is to be eaten you should instead poach them; it is a much gentler process in which the cooking liquid just moves, and the cooking is not for too long. Poached fish and meat should be tender and delicate.

Microwave cooking

With a microwave it is possible to use less fat, less cooking liquid and less salt than in conventional cooking techniques. Because it is fast it is therefore particularly convenient for dishes using grains, beans and pulses that might otherwise be very long-winded.

As a rough guide, good quality meat can be roasted on 'High' power (650 watts) but slower cooking cuts are better started off briefly on 'High' power and then cooked on 'Defrost' until tender. Recommended times are:

- 6 minutes per lb (450 g) for beef
- 6–8 minutes per lb (450 g) for lamb
- 8–10 minutes per lb (450 g) for pork

Joints for roasting should be a neat even shape, so it is a good idea to bone and roll awkward shapes if you can – or ask your butcher to do it for you. During the cooking you should remove any juices that are produced, and save them for gravy; if you leave them in the microwave they form too much steam. Place the joint on an upturned saucer so that it doesn't sit in a puddle of its own juices.

Vegetables and fruit cook quickly in a microwave, with very good results in terms of nutritional content, colour, flavour and texture. Jacket potatoes must be the biggest success story; a single potato takes a mere four minutes, while six big ones take only 20 minutes, although it is necessary to wrap them in foil whilst cooking and let them stand for a further five minutes before serving.

Containers suitable for microwave cooking include everyday china and glass, paper and bamboo, as well as plastics specially produced for the microwave. But do not use anything made of metal, dishes with a metal rim or pattern, fine bone china (it might crackle), jugs or mugs with handles glued on (the glue can melt), wood or partially glazed stoneware. But you can use *small* amounts of aluminium foil to shield parts of meat.

Pressure cooking

This technique uses an increased pressure to produce a higher than usual temperature, thus speeding the process along. The cooker can only work if there is some liquid in it to produce some steam, the minimum usually being 8 fl oz (250 ml).

It is a very good technique for robust meals such as soups, stews and vegetables for puréeing, for example, but should not be used to cook more delicate items or fresh vegetables to be served immediately.

PRESENTATION

At its most basic level food can be presented in any way – as long as there's enough and it tastes good, what does it matter? But it has to be accepted that eating involves all the senses – taste, smell, vision, texture, even hearing – so that good presentation can make a lot of difference to a meal. Not many people are going to want to elevate each and every meal to a work of art, but, on the other hand, a slovenly produced plate of food can at best be off-putting and at worst disgusting.

Garnishes provide very useful highlights with stews, casseroles and so on – meals that are usually of a uniform colour. Sprigs of parsley, mint and watercress are the most usual garnishes, but other herbs such as chervil, chives, dill, basil or flat-leaved parsley can all be appropriate. Or why not make use of slices of the various coloured peppers, or of stoned quartered olives? Slices of lemon are common accompaniments to fish, but what about slices of lime, or even of orange – orange looks and tastes very good with dark green spinach, too. A sprinkling of toasted sesame seeds (done in the microwave) can look and taste very good with many vegetables.

The preparation of the table can be as important as the preparation of the meal itself. This is not to say that each meal should involve napkins, tablecloth, glasses and the best china, but equally it doesn't take much effort to improve on slapping the cutlery in the middle of the table for everyone to help themselves. If you are making an effort to change to a low-fat diet – something that might seem quite strange at first – you can at least reward yourself and your family by spending a few seconds on the presentation.

6

BREAKFASTS

There are very sound nutritional reasons for starting the day with a meal, however quick it might have to be, especially if you are trying to reduce to a sensible weight or are trying to keep your blood cholesterol levels within healthy limits. Sadly, today many people skip breakfast, or at most have a cup of tea or coffee; consequently they tend to feel hungry later in the day and then eat biscuits, cake and other foods containing high levels of fat.

This need not be the case, though, and below we have given a wide range of ideas for breakfasts, some of them perhaps lavish, others very quick, but all of them low in fat and high in complex carbohydrates, guaranteed to keep your energy levels high throughout the day.

BREAKFAST CEREALS

There are now so many breakfast cereals on the market that it is often difficult to know what to choose. Below we give some guidelines to the different types of cereal available.

If you are trying to lose weight avoid those cereals that have a high content of refined carbohydrate, i.e. simple sugars.

Obviously this includes the sugar-coated or honey-coated cereals – stick to the plainer ones. If an examination of the ingredients list reveals sugar, sucrose, fructose, maltose, glucose (anything -ose, in fact), honey, raw cane sugar, syrup, treacle, molasses, then you should limit your consumption to occasional treats.

If you are aiming for a low-fat breakfast as well, then you should go for cereals such as cornflakes, bran flakes, oat-bran flakes, Shredded Wheat, Weetabix, Puffed Wheat and any of the oat-based cereals such as the various types of muesli available now. But try and avoid any cereals that have coconut or coconut oil listed in the ingredients, as coconut and coconut oil are very rich sources of saturated fat – the one type of fat you should be avoiding.

Porridge oats and oat bran are excellent breakfast cereals – they are complex carbohydrates with a high proportion of soluble fibre. They can either be cooked up for a hot breakfast, or eaten cold with skimmed milk and a handful of dried fruit – a do-it-yourself muesli. Alternatively you can use fresh fruit or stewed fruit as a sweetener for your cereals – the soft summer fruits such as raspberries, strawberries, blackcurrants, blackberries and loganberries are all delicious additions to breakfast cereals of any sort. And many breakfast cereals are now appearing on the market that contain a significant proportion of oat bran.

MUESLI

Nowadays you can buy all sorts of varieties of muesli, but it is more fun – and cheaper – to make your own. This is a basic recipe; once you get the hang of it you can vary the proportions and add other ingredients.

> *2 parts porridge oats*
> *2 parts jumbo oats*
> *2 parts barley flakes*
> *2 parts rye flakes*
> *1 part oat bran*
> *2 parts mixture of sultanas and seedless raisins*
> *1 part mixture of chopped hazelnuts, chopped walnuts and sunflower seeds*

Use a teacup or a mug to measure the ingredients into a large mixing bowl – a clean dry washing-up bowl might prove to be the most convenient. Rub the mixture through the fingers to separate the dried fruit and ensure all the ingredients are well mixed.

Store in airtight jars or a large plastic box, and use as required, merely adding skimmed or semi-skimmed milk to a bowlful of the muesli; with the dried fruit there should be no need for any added sugar.

PORRIDGE

In the winter you may prefer a bowl of hot porridge rather than a cold cereal.

> *1 part porridge/rolled oats*
> *2 parts water*
> *pinch of salt*

Pour the oats into a saucepan, add the water and salt and gently bring to the boil, stirring to prevent it sticking or going lumpy. Simmer over a very low heat for five minutes to allow it to cook thoroughly, then serve with skimmed milk (hot or cold) adding some fresh or tinned fruit if you prefer a sweeter taste.

Alternatively you can cook the porridge in a double boiler. There is then less chance of the mixture going lumpy, and no chance of it sticking, but it does take longer – perhaps 10 to 15 minutes altogether.

Fat content per 4 oz (100 g) serving 0.9 g
Energy content per 4 oz (100 g) serving 44 kilocalories

BREAKFAST FRUIT JUICES

So long as the fruit juices are labelled 'pure and unsweet-ened' you can choose from an ever-widening range that is now available – orange, apple, grapefruit, pineapple, grape, tomato and more. But beware of the blends of fruit flavours, as they often have sugar and water added – a quick examination of the ingredients label will reveal this if you are not sure.

BREADS, ROLLS AND CRISPBREADS

The one piece of advice here is to avoid the plain white breads and rolls, and instead go for the huge range of alternatives that have a higher proportion of complex carbohydrates and fibre:

- Wholemeal/wholegrain breads, rolls and baps.
- Wholemeal pitta bread.
- Pumpernickel.
- Rye bread.
- Rice cakes.
- Oatcakes.
- Bagels.
- Wholegrain crispbreads, e.g. wheat and sesame seed Ryvita.
- Wheat crackers enriched with bran.

SPREADS FOR YOUR BREAD

Fat spreads
The simple advice here is, if possible, to try to do without the fat spreads, such as the low-fat butter substitutes – putting butter or any other fat spread on your toast, in addition to marmalade or jam, is as much a matter of habit and social conditioning as it is taste.

However, if you feel you do need some sort of fat spread on your bread or toast, avoid the high-fat spreads, particularly those high in saturated fats, such as butter and ordinary margarine. Instead go for the very-low-fat spreads now available – try the various brands and super-market own brands until you find one that you like. And if you find it separates on hot toast, simply let the toast cool a little before spreading it. But always remember that these spreads do have an appreciable fat content, even the very-low-fat spreads, so use them sparingly – don't spread them half an inch thick as they're inclined to suggest in the advertisements.

Sweet spreads

Here we mean marmalades, jams, preserves and so on. There really is a very wide range to choose from when you include honey, malt extract, syrup, treacle, molasses, pure fruit spreads, lemon and orange curd and the fruit cheeses. Or how about mashed banana mixed with ground cinnamon/ginger/allspice and then spread on your bread or rolls?

The only proviso is, if you are aiming to reduce your weight and you want marmalade or jam, to concentrate on the reduced sugar varieties that are now available.

Savoury spreads

But why go for sweet spreads at breakfast? Why not try some savoury alternatives?

- Yeast extracts such as Marmite.
- Meat extracts such as Bovril.
- Very-low-fat curd or cottage cheeses, perhaps with tomato purée added, or mixed herbs, or chives.

You could even go for a mixture of savoury and sweet, such as very-low-fat curd or cottage cheese mixed with honey and lemon juice, or with dried fruit. Or even very-low-fat soft cheese and malt extract. The combinations are endless.

COOKED BREAKFASTS

To most people a cooked breakfast invariably means fried egg, fried bacon, sausage, fried bread and perhaps fried tomato or mushroom. And you will have realised that these are all high-fat items, and are particularly high in saturated fats. So is it goodbye to the cooked breakfast? Not at all.

BACON, TOMATO AND MUSHROOM

2 rashers very lean back bacon, visible fat removed
2 tomatoes, sliced
2oz (50g) mushrooms, sliced
1 slice wholemeal bread

Either grill the bacon, tomatoes and mushrooms, or fry them very slowly, with no added fat, in a non-stick frying pan. Serve hot on plain or toasted bread.

Serves 1
Fat content per serving 11g
Energy content per serving 303 kilocalories

HAM AND BAKED BEANS

6oz (175g) reduced sugar or no-sugar baked beans
1 tomato, sliced
1 very lean slice of ham, visible fat removed
1–2 sprigs of watercress

Heat the baked beans through in a small saucepan over gentle heat, stirring occasionally. Grill the tomato slices. Serve with the ham, garnished with watercress.

1 serving
Fat content per serving 4g
Energy content per serving 200 kilocalories

CHEESE ON TOAST WITH TOMATO

1 slice wholemeal bread
thin slices of Edam or low-fat hard cheese
2 tomatoes, sliced

Toast the bread on one side under the grill. Arrange the

slices of cheese on the untoasted side of the bread, place under the grill and cook until the cheese starts to bubble. Serve with grilled or raw slices of tomato.

1 serving
Fat content per serving 7 g
Energy content per serving 250 kilocalories

Eggs

On a low-fat diet you should be limiting yourself to a total of three to four eggs per week, including those used in cooking. So, while you won't want to have eggs every day, it does mean that you can have the occasional egg on its own, providing it is not cooked in fat or oil:

- Boiled egg.
- Poached egg.
- Scrambled egg – cooked in a microwave, scrambled egg turns out very light and fluffy.
- 'Fried' very slowly in a non-stick frying pan.
- Place an ovenproof plate over a saucepan of boiling water, crack the egg on to the plate and allow it to cook, adding other items – grilled lean bacon, slices of tomatoes, baked beans, for example – when you serve it.

An egg cooked by any of these methods, accompanied by wholemeal bread or toast, or with tomatoes, mushrooms, a rasher of really lean bacon or a low-fat sausage, plus a glass of fruit juice and a cup or two of black coffee or tea with skimmed milk, with perhaps a bowl of virtually fat-free yoghurt or low-fat fromage frais for starters, is not exactly deprivation, and will have very little impact on your fat intake.

Fish

Fish for breakfast? Why not? It's not so long ago that kippers were considered to be a breakfast speciality. Loch Fyne kippers are considered to be the best, and try to get the natural smoked kippers if possible, free from artificial colouring. If you can't cope with the bones, go for kipper fillets instead.

BREAKFAST KIPPER

1 kipper or kipper fillet
juice of $\frac{1}{2}$ a lemon
2 tomatoes, sliced
1 teaspoon freshly chopped parsley

Place the kipper or kipper fillet under a preheated moderately hot grill, skin side up, for five minutes. Turn and cook the other side for five minutes. Alternatively, place it on a baking tray, cover with greaseproof paper or aluminium foil and place in a preheated oven, gas mark 4 (180°C, 350°F) for 10–15 minutes or until heated through. Sprinkle the lemon juice over the kipper, and serve with grilled tomato slices strewn with chopped parsley.

Serves 1
Fat content per serving 17 g
Energy content per serving 339 kilocalories

OTHER BREAKFAST IDEAS

Why stick to the more traditional ideas for breakfast? Why not try some of the following?

- Scones (Chapter 12) with sweet or savoury toppings.
- Drop scones (Chapter 12). Make the mixture the night before and have the scones freshly cooked for breakfast, topped with a little honey or jam.
- Stuffed pancakes. Again, make up the mixture (Chapter 8) the night before and have the pancakes freshly cooked – perhaps spread with honey or maple syrup, or even stuffed with very-low-fat curd or cottage cheese and jam.
- Have a bowl of dried prunes or dried apricots (Hunza apricots are the best) soaked overnight in apple juice and topped with plain virtually-fat-free fromage frais.

7

LIGHT MEALS

SNACKS

LEAN BURGERS

For this recipe you need best-quality lean minced beef.
Once you've got used to making your own burgers you'll
wonder why you ever had any other.

> 1 lb (450 g) very lean minced beef
> 1 onion, chopped
> 1 green or red pepper, cored, deseeded and chopped
> 1 clove garlic, crushed
> 1/2 teaspoon cayenne pepper
> 2 teaspoons soy sauce
> 1 tablespoon tomato purée
> 2 tablespoons wholemeal breadcrumbs
> 1 egg

Mix all the ingredients together in the bowl and leave to
stand for two hours. Divide into six equal portions, shape
into burgers and cook immediately under a preheated
grill, or over a barbecue on a close-meshed wire rack or
metal sheet. Alternatively, once you have shaped the
burgers they can be frozen and used at a later date.

Makes 6 burgers
Fat content per burger 5 g
Energy content per burger 121 kilocalories

BEAN BURGERS

An equally tasty alternative to meat burgers are these bean burgers.

> *6 oz (175 g) red kidney beans*
> *4 oz (100 g) butter beans*
> *4 oz (100 g) porridge oats*
> *1 onion, chopped*
> *1 red pepper, cored, deseeded and chopped*
> *1 clove garlic, crushed*
> *1 tablespoon Marmite*
> *4 tablespoons tomato ketchup*
> *1 teaspoon Dijon mustard*
> *½ teaspoon ground ginger*
> *1 egg*
> *freshly milled black pepper*
> *wholemeal flour for dusting*

Place the kidney beans and butter beans in two large bowls, cover with cold water and leave to soak overnight. Drain the beans, put them in two large saucepans, cover with cold water and bring to the boil. Reduce the heat and simmer until the skins are splitting; in a pressure cooker this will take about 10 minutes at full pressure with the 15 lb weight.

Drain the cooked beans. Combine them in a bowl and mash to a pulp with a wooden spoon or potato masher. Stir in the remaining ingredients, mixing well. Put the mixture in the refrigerator for two hours to allow it to stiffen.

Divide the mixture into six equal portions and shape into burgers, using a little wholemeal flour to dust the burgers and prevent the mixture sticking to your hands. Cook under a preheated grill, or over a barbecue on a fine-mesh wire rack or metal sheet. Alternatively they can be frozen and used at a later date.

Makes 6 burgers
Fat content per burger 3 g
Energy content per burger 147 kilocalories

HASLET

This is a very old recipe that needs no amendment to make it low in fat. Haslet can be sliced and served cold with salad, or the slices warmed on a large plate and served with jacket potatoes.

> *8 oz (225 g) stale wholemeal bread*
> *skimmed milk*
> *2 lb (1 kg) very lean pork, visible fat removed, coarsely minced*
> *1 large onion, chopped*
> *1 teaspoon freshly chopped sage*
> *1 teaspoon freshly chopped thyme*
> *$^1/_2$ teaspoon freshly ground black pepper*
> *pinch of salt*

Break the stale bread into small lumps, place in a bowl and pour over enough skimmed milk to cover. Leave to soak, and when the bread has softened, remove it from the milk and squeeze out the excess moisture.

In a mixing bowl combine the bread, minced pork, onion, herbs and seasonings. Transfer the mixture to a food processor and work to a fine consistency. Alternatively feed the mixture through the fine blade of a mincing machine. Spoon into a greased loaf tin lined with greaseproof paper and bake in a preheated oven, gas mark 5 (190°C, 375°F) for $1^1/_2$ hours. Allow to cool, turn out on to a wire rack and, when quite cold, remove the greaseproof paper.

Makes up to 20 slices
Fat content per slice 4 g
Energy content per slice 95 kilocalories

POTATO CAKES

These make an excellent accompaniment to a light meal, or can be served on their own topped with baked beans, tomatoes and onion rings, a spoonful of fromage frais and chutney, or whatever else you choose.

1 lb (450 g) potatoes, peeled, cooked and drained
1 oz (25 g) sunflower margarine
4 oz (100 g) wholemeal flour, sifted
salt and black pepper

Break up the potatoes with a fork, then push through a sieve into a mixing bowl. Beat the margarine into the sieved potatoes. Sprinkle over the flour, forking it in to combine the ingredients smoothly. Knead the mixture well and season to taste.

Roll the potato dough out on to a floured board until it is $1/2$ inch (1 cm) thick. Cut into 3-inch (7.5-cm) rounds with a pastry cutter. Wipe the base of a frying pan or griddle with kitchen paper soaked in mono-unsaturated or polyunsaturated oil. Place over moderate heat and cook the cakes for about three minutes on each side.

Makes 12–16 cakes
Fat content per cake 2 g
Energy content per cake 72 kilocalories

SANDWICHES

This section includes a number of ideas for sandwich fillings that are moist enough to be used without any butter, margarine or low-fat spread. As you can see, there is a wide variety of ideas – after all, variety is the key to a diet that is not only enjoyable but is also one you're going to want to stick to.

Many of the sandwich fillings are based on:

• Very-low-fat cottage cheese.

- Very-low-fat curd cheese.
- Virtually fat-free plain yoghurt.
- Virtually fat-free plain fromage frais.

After a time you will find that these are standard items in your refrigerator.

For the sandwich bases, avoid white bread if possible. Instead go for:

- Wholemeal, rye, granary or multigrain breads.
- Crusty wholemeal rolls and baps.
- Wholemeal French bread.
- Wholemeal pitta bread.
- Pumpernickel, or other continental wholegrain breads.
- Rice or oatcakes.

Sandwich fillings

- A little very-low-fat curd cheese, a sliced tomato, sliced raw mushroom dipped in lemon juice and slice of lean ham.
- A slice of lean ham plus a 1-inch (2.5-cm) cube of Edam or low-fat hard cheese, grated, and a sliced tomato.
- A slice of lean ham, chopped and mixed with two tablespoons plain virtually fat-free fromage frais and one teaspoon Dijon mustard, on a bed of shredded red cabbage.
- Cooked diced chicken breast, diced red or green pepper, a chopped pineapple ring, one teaspoon tomato purée, all mixed with sufficient plain virtually fat-free yoghurt to moisten.
- Some diced cooked chicken breast mixed with one tablespoon plain virtually fat-free fromage frais, one teaspoon tomato purée and a little curry paste.
- Cooked diced chicken or turkey breast stirred into some very-low-fat soft cheese, with slices of kiwi fruit or peach.
- Cooked diced chicken breast mixed with one

73

teaspoon tomato purée, a pinch of chilli powder and some shredded lettuce.

- Diced cooked chicken breast mixed with half a diced peach, one tablespoon virtually fat-free plain yoghurt, a little curry paste and a few drops of Tabasco sauce.
- Spread your bread with tomato purée, add a bed of shredded lettuce and top with a rasher of lean well-grilled back bacon, visible fat removed.
- Remove all the visible fat from a 3-oz (75-g) steak and grill it well. Slice thinly and arrange the slices on the bread of your choice. Spread with mustard and add slices of tomato.
- A slice of lean roast beef, visible fat removed, chopped and mixed with a little plain virtually fat-free fromage frais, one teaspoon horseradish sauce, a little mustard, served on a bed of shredded lettuce.
- One tablespoon diced cold roast pork mixed with one small chopped apple, a little lemon juice, one table-spoon virtually fat-free plain yoghurt and one teaspoon mixed chopped walnuts and raisins.
- Three tinned sardines in tomato sauce, mashed, plus sliced tomato.
- Mashed tuna mixed with chopped green pepper and chopped cucumber, on a bed of shredded lettuce.
- Some cooked, skinned and mashed mackerel, mixed with some very-low-fat soft cheese, lemon juice and black pepper.
- Grated 1-inch (2.5-cm) cube of Edam or low-fat hard cheese mixed with Dijon mustard, one tablespoon virtually fat-free plain yoghurt and black pepper.
- Grated 1-inch (2.5-cm) cube of Edam or low-fat hard cheese mixed with very-low-fat cottage cheese, chopped celery and Worcestershire sauce.
- Cooked chickpeas, mashed, mixed with virtually fat-free plain yoghurt, lemon juice and black pepper.
- Grated raw carrot, one tablespoon sultanas/raisins, one tablespoon orange juice and one tablespoon virtually fat-free plain yoghurt.
- Grated raw white cabbage, carrot and celery, one

chopped pineapple ring, one tablespoon peanuts and raisins, mixed with one tablespoon virtually fat-free plain fromage frais.

- A slice of lean cooked pork, one mashed pineapple ring, sliced tomatoes and a little mustard.
- Very-low-fat cottage cheese mixed with finely grated carrot, one tablespoon raisins, a dash of lemon juice and two teaspoons finely chopped onion.
- Mashed cooked red beans mixed with chopped red, green and yellow peppers, chopped onions and black pepper.
- Mashed cooked green lentils mixed with chopped onions and crushed garlic, on slices of tomato.
- A slice of well-grilled lean back bacon, thin slices of Brie or Camembert, topped with watercress and grated carrot.
- A small ripe banana mashed with a little lemon juice, one tablespoon sultanas and two tablespoons very-low-fat cottage cheese.

And now a few sweet sandwich fillings:

- One tablespoon chopped stoned dates, one table-spoon raisins, one tablespoon chopped dried apricots, mixed with very-low-fat cottage cheese. If you like you can add a pinch or two of curry powder to turn this into a savoury sandwich mix.
- A thin spreading of peanut butter, topped with a mashed banana sprinkled with lemon juice.
- A thin spreading of peanut butter topped with finely chopped or grated apple and sprinkled with lemon juice.
- One stick of celery, finely chopped, one tablespoon chopped dried apricots, one tablespoon chopped stoned dates, half an apple, grated, one tablespoon sunflower seeds, all mixed with plain virtually fat-free fromage frais.
- Thin slices of Brie, banana and cucumber, sprinkled with lemon juice.

KIPPER AND CURD CHEESE
Finally, a slightly more elaborate sandwich filling.

> *1 kipper fillet*
> *8 oz (225 g) low-fat curd cheese*
> *2 tablespoons plain virtually fat-free yoghurt*
> *2 teaspoons horseradish sauce*
> *½ teaspoon lemon juice*
> *freshly ground black pepper to taste*
> *1 tablespoon chopped onion or chives*

Remove the skin from the kipper fillet and discard. Mash the flesh in a bowl, removing any tiny bones you come across. Add the remaining ingredients and mix with a fork until the texture is smooth and creamy.

Makes 16–20 servings
Fat content per serving 4 g
Energy content per serving 43 kilocalories

CHUTNEYS AND PICKLES

Chutneys and pickles can be mixed with all sorts of other additions to make tasty moist sandwich fillings. Alternatively, they can be used as additions to all sorts of meals, from snacks to salads.

GREEN TOMATO CHUTNEY
There are many and varied recipes for green tomato chutney – this one is quite spicy.

> *1½ lb (750 g) green tomatoes*
> *1½–2 lb (750 g–1 kg) cooking apples, peeled and cored weight*
> *1½ lb (750 g) shallots, chopped*
> *1 lb (450 g) sultanas*
> *1 lb (450 g) brown sugar*
> *1 teaspoon salt*

½ teaspoon pepper
1 teaspoon ground ginger
8 cloves
6 dried red chilli peppers
1 pint (600 ml) malt vinegar

Mince the tomatoes, apple and shallots or chop them very finely. Place in a large saucepan or preserving pan and add all the remaining ingredients, except the vinegar. Bring to the boil over a moderate heat, stirring occasionally. Boil, uncovered, for one hour.

Add the malt vinegar and bring back to the boil. Reduce the heat and simmer for two to three hours until the chutney has become quite thick, by which time you will have about 7 lb (3 kg) of chutney – the precise amount will depend on how long you have simmered it for.

Spoon into warm dry jars, seal and leave for at least two weeks before using.

BANANA CHUTNEY
The disadvantage of most chutney recipes is that you have to simmer the mixture for ages. In contrast, this chutney can be made in half an hour. Furthermore, if you ask for brown squidgy bananas you can often get them for next to nothing.

12 brown bananas, peeled and chopped
1 pint (600 ml) malt vinegar
6 oz (175 g) seedless raisins
6 oz (175 g) stoned dates, chopped
6 oz (175 g) shallots, chopped
8 oz (225 g) muscovado/dark brown sugar
1 teaspoon salt
2 teaspoons coriander seeds
1 tablespoon ground cinnamon
1 tablespoon turmeric

Put the chopped bananas in a large saucepan with the vinegar. Bring to the boil, reduce the heat and simmer for five minutes until the mixture has thickened.

Add the remaining ingredients, stir well and bring back to the boil. Simmer for 15 minutes. This will make 4½–5½lb (2–2.5kg) of chutney.

Spoon into warm dry jars, seal and keep for at least two weeks before using.

MARROW CHUTNEY

This is a hotter chutney than the two previous recipes.

> *4lb (1.75kg) marrow (peeled, deseeded and chopped weight)*
> *salt*
> *12oz (350g) chopped onion or shallots*
> *10 cloves*
> *2 teaspoons turmeric*
> *1 tablespoon ground ginger*
> *1 tablespoon mustard powder*
> *10 red chilli peppers*
> *1lb (450g) granulated sugar*
> *2 pints (1.25 litres) white malt vinegar*

Place the marrow chunks in a large colander. Sprinkle with plenty of salt and leave overnight to sweat. Rinse, then drain off the liquid thoroughly in the colander.

Put all the other ingredients in a large saucepan or preserving pan and bring up to the boil. Boil for 10–15 minutes, add the marrow and boil for a further 30–40 minutes, or until the marrow is soft. Like the green tomato chutney, the exact amount of chutney you are left with depends on how long you simmer the mixture, but this recipe should make approximately 6½lb (3kg).

Ladle into clean warm dry jars, seal and leave for two weeks before using.

PACKED LUNCHES

More and more people are making use of packed lunches nowadays – not just schoolchildren, but people whose work involves a lot of travelling around by car, people who may not have access to a canteen or restaurant, or simply people who don't want the expense or the extra-vagance of a sit-down meal at lunch time.

We have seen that the humble sandwich – the basis of most packed lunches – can be both exciting and nutritious. But why stick to traditional sandwiches, when you could try some of these:

- Wholemeal pitta bread filled with one of the sandwich fillings described above.
- Wholemeal pitta bread filled with one of the salads described in Chapter 11.
- Pancakes rolled up around a sandwich or salad filling.
- A cold jacket potato with a tub of salad, sandwich filling or a dip to have with it.
- A double-decker sandwich with sandwich filling in the lower section and perhaps a salad in the upper section.

Or you could forget about sandwiches completely. Take a pot of salad with you, or a pot of cold cooked vegetables – ratatouille (Chapter 11), for example, tastes as good cold the next day as it does hot.

At any time of year there is always plenty of fresh fruit to choose from, so you can add to your packed lunch peaches, nectarines, plums, greengages in the summer; apples and pears in the autumn and winter; bananas and oranges all the year round; satsumas, tangerines and clementines in the spring. Or take some dried fruit as well – dates, apricots, figs, apple rings, pear slices, for example.

Raw vegetables can also enliven a packed lunch, perhaps with a pot of savoury dip to accompany them. Always available are:

- Tomatoes.
- Lengths of celery stick.
- Chunks of cucumber.
- Cauliflower florets.
- Rings cut from young sweetcorn – corn on the cob. If the corn is young enough, not only can you eat the sweetcorn kernels, but also the cob.
- Carrots, whole or in chunks.
- Radishes.

Pots of virtually fat-free yoghurt and fromage frais are readily available now from all the supermarket chains, and make a very good addition to a packed lunch, particularly as you can buy them natural or fruit-flavoured. Better still, buy a natural one and chop fresh fruit into it.

Then there are thermos flask lunches. Thermos flasks are now produced in all sorts of designs, shapes and sizes, from huge ones for picnics down to individual tubby ones designed to take a single portion of hot soup, stew or casserole. So if you have some leftover soup, why not heat it up before you leave for work, pour it into the thermos and treat yourself to a hot packed lunch?

Clearly there's more to packed lunches than a cheese sandwich, a packet of crisps, a Mars bar and an apple. After experimenting with some of our suggestions, you'll be able to dream up all sorts of interesting and tasty combinations, and all of them low in fat.

8

FAMILY MEALS

SOUPS

JERUSALEM ARTICHOKE SOUP

Jerusalem artichokes discolour rapidly once they have been peeled. After they have been peeled, drop them into water to which you have added a dash of vinegar or lemon juice.

> *1 teaspoon mono-unsaturated or polyunsaturated oil*
> *2 onions, chopped*
> *4 sticks celery, chopped*
> *1½lb (750g) Jerusalem artichokes, peeled and chopped*
> *1½ pints (900ml) skimmed milk*
> *½ pint (300ml) medium white wine*
> *1 bay leaf*
> *3 blades of mace*
> *pinch of salt*
> *pinch of pepper*
> *sprig of parsley, chopped, to garnish*

In a large saucepan heat the oil and fry the onions gently until they are soft and golden. Add the celery and artichoke. Continue cooking for another five minutes, stirring occasionally. Add the milk, wine, bay leaf, mace and seasoning and bring to the boil. Reduce the heat and

81

simmer gently for 30 minutes.

Remove the bay leaf and the mace. Transfer the soup to a blender or food processor, working in batches if necessary, and work to a purée. Return to a clean saucepan and bring back up to heat. Serve with a sprinkling of chopped parsley.

Serves 4
Fat content per serving 2 g
Energy content per serving 197 kilocalories

RICH LENTIL AND SPLIT PEA SOUP

Once you get used to making this basic recipe you can add different vegetables, and vary the proportions and types of lentils and split peas. Leek tops and green split peas make a delicious variation. If you use dried herbs, halve the quantities.

> *1/2 teaspoon mono-unsaturated or polyunsaturated oil*
> *1 large onion, chopped*
> *4 sticks celery, chopped*
> *3 pints (1.75 litres) vegetable or chicken stock*
> *8 oz (225 g) red lentils*
> *8 oz (225 g) yellow split peas*
> *1 clove garlic, crushed*
> *2 bay leaves*
> *2 teaspoons freshly chopped mixed herbs*
> *salt and pepper to taste*

Heat the oil in a large saucepan and fry the onion over moderate heat, stirring frequently, until it is golden brown. Add the celery and stir-fry for one to two minutes more. Add the stock and the remaining ingredients. Bring to the boil and simmer for one to two hours, stirring occasionally. In a pressure cooker this will take 30 minutes at full pressure with the 15 lb weight.

Remove the bay leaves from the soup, and mash the vegetables with a potato masher. The texture should not be over-refined. The soup can then be served immediately, although it improves if left to stand for a few hours and then reheated.

Serves 6
Fat content per serving 2 g
Energy content per serving 245 kilocalories

SPICY LENTIL SOUP

1 lb (450 g) green lentils, washed
4 medium onions, chopped
5 pints (2.75 litres) water
1 teaspoon ground coriander
1/2 teaspoon ground ginger
2 bay leaves
salt and black pepper to taste
6 tablespoons plain virtually fat-free yoghurt or fromage frais
6 sprigs fresh coriander, to garnish

Put all the ingredients except the yoghurt or fromage frais and the coriander sprigs into a large heavy-bottomed saucepan set over moderate heat. Bring to the boil and simmer for 45 minutes to one hour or until the lentils are quite tender. Pour into bowls and serve with a swirl of yoghurt or fromage frais and a sprig of coriander on top.

Serves 6
Fat content per serving 1 g
Energy content per serving 259 kilocalories

TOMATO AND CHICKPEA SOUP

1/2 teaspoon mono-unsaturated or polyunsaturated oil
1 onion, chopped
1 clove garlic, crushed
1 × 14 oz (400 g) can tomatoes
1 × 14 oz (400 g) can chickpeas, drained and rinsed
1 pint (600 ml) vegetable stock
salt and black pepper

Heat the oil in a large saucepan and fry the onion gently

until soft and golden. Add the garlic and cook for another two minutes, then add the tomatoes, chickpeas and stock. Bring to the boil and simmer for 30 minutes. Allow to cool slightly then transfer the soup to a blender or processor. Work to a smooth consistency. Return to the saucepan and heat through. Season to taste and serve.

Serves 6
Fat content per serving 3 g
Energy content per serving 115 kilocalories

STARTERS

STUFFED TOMATOES

 4 large firm tomatoes
 2 oz (50 g) chopped walnuts
 2 sticks celery, finely chopped
 1 teaspoon soy sauce
 1 teaspoon dark brown sugar
 salt and freshly milled black pepper

Carefully slice off the top of each tomato and scoop out the pulp into a bowl. To the pulp add the chopped walnuts and celery, the soy sauce and the sugar, and mix well. Carefully spoon the mixture back into the tomatoes and replace the tops. Place on a baking sheet in a preheated oven, gas mark 5 (190°C, 375°F), for 15 minutes. Serve hot.

Serves 4
Fat content per serving 7 g
Energy content per serving 102 kilocalories

SMOKED HADDOCK COCKTAIL

 8 oz (225 g) smoked haddock fillet, skinned
 ¼ pint (150 ml) skimmed milk
 ¼ pint (150 ml) tomato ketchup
 1 teaspoon Worcestershire sauce
 1 tablespoon horseradish sauce

pinch of mustard powder
2 tablespoons very-low-fat soft cheese
1 tablespoon plain virtually fat-free yoghurt
1 lettuce, washed and shredded
1 tablespoon freshly chopped parsley

Place the haddock in a saucepan, cover with the skimmed milk and set over a gentle heat. When the milk just comes to the boil, reduce the heat to very low and poach the fish for five minutes, or until the flesh flakes easily. Do not overcook. Lift out the fish, discarding the milk, and flake the flesh into a bowl. Leave to cool. In another bowl combine the tomato ketchup, Worcestershire sauce, horseradish sauce and mustard with the cheese and yoghurt. Fold in the flaked haddock and stir lightly.

Arrange the shredded lettuce in serving bowls and spoon over the haddock mixture. To serve, garnish with the chopped parsley.

Serves 6
Fat content per serving 1 g
Energy content per serving 89 kilocalories

SHRIMP AND APPLE SURPRISE

The slightly piquant tomato sauce makes a delicious contrast to the shrimp and chopped apple.

frisée lettuce and radicchio leaves, shredded
1 lemon, halved
6 tablespoons plain virtually fat-free fromage frais
2 teaspoons tomato purée
1/2 teaspoon Worcestershire sauce
2 crisp dessert apples, peeled, cored and chopped
2 sticks celery, chopped
4 oz (100 g) shrimps, cooked, peeled and halved
pinch of pepper

Arrange a bed of lettuce and radicchio leaves as a bed on each of four serving plates or bowls, and squeeze over the juice of one half of the lemon. Cut the remaining half lemon into slices.

In a bowl mix together the fromage frais, tomato purée and Worcestershire sauce. Add the apple, celery and shrimps and season to taste. Pile the mixture over the salad leaves and garnish with lemon slices to serve.

Serves 4
Fat content per serving 2g
Energy content per serving 69 kilocalories

VEGETARIAN NUT PÂTÉ

> 2 oz (50 g) chopped hazelnuts
> 2 oz (50 g) chopped walnuts
> 2 oz (50 g) chopped cashew nuts
> 1/2 teaspoon mono-unsaturated or polyunsaturated oil
> 1 onion, finely chopped
> 4 oz (100 g) mushrooms, finely chopped
> 1 clove garlic, crushed
> 2 teaspoons tomato purée
> 1 tablespoon medium oatmeal
> 6 tablespoons white wine or medium sherry
> 2 teaspoons soy sauce
> 1 teaspoon freshly chopped thyme
> 2 oz (50 g) porridge oats
> 1 egg, beaten
> freshly milled black pepper
> 3 bay leaves

Grind the nuts in a clean coffee grinder or food processor, or pass them through the fine blade of a mincer. Set aside.

In a large saucepan heat the oil and cook the onion gently until soft and transparent. Add the mushrooms and garlic and cook for another five minutes, then stir in the tomato purée. Sprinkle the oatmeal over the mixture, then add the wine or sherry, soy sauce and thyme. Stir well to combine and add the ground nuts and porridge oats. Mix in the egg and black pepper to taste.

Line a 1 lb (450 g) loaf tin with greaseproof paper, and arrange the bay leaves in the bottom of the tin. Spoon in the pâté, making sure the corners are filled, and smooth the top level. Cover with aluminium foil or greaseproof paper. Place the tin in a baking tray one-third full of boiling water and bake in a preheated oven, gas mark 4 (180°C, 350°F) for one hour. Turn out on to a wire rack and leave to cool. When cold, remove the greaseproof paper, leaving the bay leaves in place.

Serves 6
Fat content per serving 14 g
Energy content per serving 204 kilocalories

MUSHROOMS AND GARLIC IN YOGHURT
In this recipe it is important not to overcook the mushrooms, otherwise they lose their flavour.

> *1 lb (450 g) button mushrooms*
> *1/2 oz (15 g) sunflower margarine*
> *salt and freshly milled black pepper*
> *3 cloves garlic, crushed*
> *pinch of freshly grated nutmeg or ground nutmeg*
> *1 tablespoon freshly chopped parsley*
> *4 tablespoons virtually fat-free plain yoghurt*

Wipe the mushrooms clean with kitchen paper. Trim the stalks if necessary. Heat the margarine in a large frying pan. Add the mushrooms and cook gently for two to three minutes, stirring occasionally. Add the salt and pepper, garlic, nutmeg and parsley, and continue to cook for two to three minutes longer shaking the pan so that nothing sticks. Finally add the yoghurt and cook gently for five minutes. Serve immediately.

Serves 4
Fat content per serving 4 g
Energy content per serving 50 kilocalories

VEGETABLE QUICHE

8 oz (225 g) oat pastry (see page 172)
1 carrot, grated
1 small red pepper, cored, deseeded and diced
1 small green pepper, cored, deseeded and diced
1 yellow pepper, cored, deseeded and diced
1 onion, sliced into half rings
2 oz (50 g) mushrooms, sliced
2–3 tomatoes, sliced
½ pint (300 ml) skimmed milk
2 egg whites
1 teaspoon freshly chopped thyme
salt and freshly milled black pepper

Grease a 8½-inch (22-cm) flan dish. Line it with oat pastry and bake blind as described on page 172. Allow to cool.

Strew the vegetables evenly and attractively inside the pastry shell. In a bowl beat together the milk, egg whites, thyme and seasoning. Pour this mixture over the vegetables. Bake in a preheated oven, gas mark 5 (190°C, 375°F) for about 30 minutes or until the quiche has just started to brown. Serve hot or cold.

Serves 8
Fat content per serving 12 g
Energy content per serving 217 kilocalories

MAIN COURSES

LENTIL ROAST
This is an extremely tasty dish based on lentils. Once you have got used to cooking it you can introduce flavourings other than soy sauce or Marmite – add a dash of Worcestershire sauce for example – and vary the herbs.

8 oz (225 g) red lentils
¾ pint (450 ml) water

> 2 small or 1 large onion, chopped
> 1 teaspoon soy sauce or Marmite
> 1 × 1¼-oz (50-g) tin anchovies
> 1 tablespoon freshly chopped mixed herbs
> 1 egg
> 1–2 tomatoes, sliced

Place the lentils, water, chopped onion and soy sauce or Marmite in a heavy-bottomed saucepan. Bring to the boil and simmer for 15–20 minutes until the lentils are soft. Leave to stand for another five to 10 minutes until the lentils are completely mushy.

Place half the anchovies in a small bowl and mash with a fork to a coarse purée. Beat into the lentil mixture and add the herbs and the egg.

Pour the mixture into a well-greased 8½-inch (22-cm) flan dish. Decorate with the sliced tomato and the remaining anchovies and bake in a preheated oven, gas mark 4 (180°C, 350°F) for 30–40 minutes.

Serves 4
Fat content per serving 5 g
Energy content per serving 227 kilocalories

BOSTON BAKED BEANS

This is an exciting way to create your own baked bean dish. You need to get lean pork – spare rib chops, fillet or tenderloin, if you can afford it – and trim off any visible fat before cooking.

> 2 lb (900 g) mixture of red kidney and haricot beans
> 4 pints (2.5 litres) water
> 8 oz (225 g) lean pork, chopped
> 1 onion, chopped
> 3 tablespoons black treacle
> 2 tablespoons brown sugar
> 1 teaspoon mustard powder
> 1 teaspoon salt

Soak the beans for a minimum of six hours, or preferably

overnight, in a bowl of cold water. Drain the beans and place them in a large saucepan with the measured water. Cook slowly until the skins start to burst; if you are using a pressure cooker this takes 10 minutes at full pressure using the 15 lb weight.

Drain the beans, reserving the cooking water, and transfer them to a deep casserole. Bury the pieces of pork among the beans.

Place the chopped onion, treacle, sugar, mustard powder and salt in a small saucepan with $1/2$ pint (300 ml) of the reserved cooking water and mix together. Bring to the boil, then pour over the beans and pork in the casserole. Add enough of the remaining reserved water to just cover the beans, put the lid on the casserole and cook in a preheated oven, at gas mark 3 (160°C, 325°F) for 3–4 hours. Remove the lid for the last half hour of cooking to crisp the top.

Serves 6
Fat content per serving 6 g
Energy content per serving 244 kilocalories

RED BEAN LOAF

This nutritious main meal can be served either hot or cold, with or without an accompanying sauce.

> *7 oz (200 g) red kidney beans*
> *$1/2$ teaspoon mono-unsaturated or polyunsaturated oil*
> *2 medium onions, chopped*
> *1 red or green pepper, cored, deseeded and chopped*
> *50 g (2 oz) plain shelled peanuts, chopped*
> *4 oz (100 g) rolled oats*
> *2 cloves garlic, crushed*
> *1 tablespoon soy sauce or Marmite*
> *1 tablespoon tomato ketchup*
> *1 teaspoon freshly chopped thyme*
> *pinch of chilli powder*
> *pinch of salt*
> *pinch of pepper*

Soak the beans in cold water for at least six hours, and preferably overnight. Drain, place in a saucepan and cover with fresh water. Bring to the boil and simmer until the skins start splitting; if you are using a pressure cooker this takes about 10 minutes at full pressure using the 15 lb weight.

Drain the cooked beans, tip into a mixing bowl and mash to a paste. Heat the oil in a saucepan and fry the onion, pepper and peanuts until the vegetables are soft. Add to the mashed bean paste. Add the remaining ingredients, stirring with a fork to combine well.

Line a 1 lb (450 g) loaf tin with greaseproof paper and spoon in the mixture, smoothing the top level. Bake in a preheated oven, gas mark 7 (220°C, 425°F), for 30–45 minutes – the top of the loaf should be firm and brown. Remove from the oven and allow to cool in the tin for five to 10 minutes. Turn the loaf out of the tin and remove the greaseproof paper.

Serves 6
Fat content per serving 7 g
Energy content per serving 168 kilocalories

SMOKED FISH COTTAGE PIE
This is a somewhat more interesting variation on the basic fish cottage pie.

2 lb (1 kg) peeled potatoes
1/2 pint (300 ml) skimmed milk
1 1/2 lb (750 g) smoked cod fillets, skinned
1 bay leaf
1 tablespoon cornflour
1 clove garlic, crushed
1 bunch fresh parsley, chopped
pinch of salt
pinch of pepper
1 oz (25 g) peanuts, chopped

Boil the potatoes until cooked, drain and mash with one

tablespoon of the milk. Set to one side and keep warm.

Place the fish in a large saucepan with the remaining milk and the bay leaf. Poach over gentle heat for five to 10 minutes. Drain the fish, reserving the milk but discarding the bay leaf. Flake the fish, removing any bones, and place in an ovenproof dish.

Put the cornflour in a teacup, add some of the reserved milk (it should be no more than warm) and stir to a cream. Pour the remaining milk into a clean saucepan, add the cornflour paste mixture and bring to the boil, stirring constantly until the sauce thickens. Add the garlic, chopped parsley, salt and pepper.

Pour the parsley sauce over the flaked fish and mix gently. Carefully cover with a layer of mashed potato. Sprinkle with chopped peanuts and bake in a preheated oven, gas mark 4 (180°C, 350°F), for 20 minutes. Finally, place under a hot grill for three to five minutes to brown the top.

Serves 4
Fat content per serving 5 g
Energy content per serving 402 kilocalories

KEDGEREE

Another smoked fish dish, this time based on rice.

1¹/₂ lb (750 g) smoked haddock fillet, skinned
¹/₂ pint (300 ml) skimmed milk
10 oz (275 g) brown rice
¹/₂ pint (300 ml) water
¹/₂ teaspoon mono-unsaturated or polyunsaturated oil
2 oz (50 g) cashew nuts, chopped
pinch of salt
pinch of grated nutmeg
pinch of ground chilli pepper
2 teaspoons lemon juice
4 oz (100 g) plain virtually fat-free yoghurt
1 tablespoon freshly chopped parsley

Place the haddock in a large saucepan, pour on the milk and bring slowly to the boil. Reduce the heat and simmer for five to 10 minutes until the haddock falls apart easily. Drain the fish, reserving the milk.

Put the rice into a saucepan, add the milk and the water, bring to the boil and simmer for 25 minutes with the lid on. Remove from the heat and allow to stand, but do not remove the lid. After 10 minutes the rice will be cooked.

Heat the oil in a small pan and fry the cashew nuts, taking care not to burn them – they should be light gold, not dark brown.

Flake the fish into a large bowl, removing any bones. Turn the cooked rice into the bowl, together with the salt, nutmeg, pepper, chilli pepper, lemon juice, yoghurt, cashews and most of the parsley. Combine the ingredients well and transfer to a large ovenproof dish. Cover and bake in a preheated oven, gas mark 4 (180°C, 350°F), for 30 minutes. Remove the lid, sprinkle with the remaining chopped parsley and serve.

Serves 6
Fat content per serving 7 g
Energy content per serving 359 kilocalories

LENTIL STEW WITH SHREDDED CABBAGE

> 9oz (250g) brown lentils
> 1/2 teaspoon mono-unsaturated or polyunsaturated oil
> 1 medium onion, chopped
> 2 carrots, chopped
> 1 small leek, chopped
> 1 large tomato, roughly chopped
> 1 pint (600ml) vegetable stock
> 1 clove garlic, crushed
> 1 small savoy cabbage, blanched, squeezed and shredded
> 2 teaspoons wine vinegar
> 1 tablespoon freshly chopped flat-leaf parsley
> salt and freshly milled black pepper

Wash the lentils thoroughly in a bowl of cold water, picking out any stems and lentils that float to the surface. Drain.

Heat the oil in a flameproof casserole and cook the onion for three to four minutes. Add the carrots, leek and tomato and cook for a further three to four minutes. Add the stock, garlic and well-drained lentils and bring to the boil. Simmer for about 20 minutes, or until the lentils are just soft.

Remove about a quarter of the vegetable and lentil mixture and liquidise in a blender or processor. Return this purée to the casserole, add the shredded cabbage and stir. Finally add the vinegar and parsley, and season to taste.

Serves 4
Fat content per serving 1 g
Energy content per serving 137 kilocalories

GRILLED FILLET OF COD

6 cod fillets, each weighing 4–6 oz (100–175 g)
2 oz (50 g) wholemeal flour or
1 oz (25 g) plain flour and 1 oz (25 g) wholemeal flour
salt and black pepper
1 tablespoon mono-unsaturated or polyunsaturated oil
juice of 1 lemon
2 tablespoons freshly chopped parsley
To garnish:
6 lemon wedges
4 tomatoes, sliced

Wash the fish, removing the skin if necessary, and pat dry with kitchen paper.

Mix the flour and seasoning and use to coat both sides of each fillet. Place the fillets on a non-stick tray, dribble over the oil and cook for 10–15 minutes under a preheated hot grill until golden brown, turning once or twice. Sprinkle lemon juice over the fish as it cooks.

Sprinkle with chopped parsley before serving and garnish with lemon wedges and tomato slices.

Serves 6
Fat content per serving 4 g
Energy content per serving 221 kilocalories

CHICKEN AND SWEETCORN CASSEROLE

> *1 tablespoon mono-unsaturated or polyunsaturated oil*
> *4 skinless, boneless chicken portions*
> *1 onion, chopped*
> *1 small green pepper, cored, deseeded and chopped*
> *3 oz (75 g) carrots, scrubbed and sliced*
> *2 oz (50 g) button mushrooms, sliced*
> *1 oz (25 g) wholemeal flour*
> *2 tablespoons tomato purée*
> *1 pint (600 ml) chicken or vegetable stock*
> *3 oz (75 g) tomatoes, sliced*
> *6 oz (175 g) sweetcorn kernels, canned or frozen*
> *salt and black pepper*
> *1 tablespoon freshly chopped parsley, to garnish*

Heat the oil in a heavy-bottomed saucepan over a moderate heat, add the chicken pieces and cook, turning them over until they are browned and sealed. Remove the chicken and place in a casserole.

In the remaining oil fry the chopped onion until soft. Add the pepper and carrots and cook for another five to 10 minutes. Finally add the mushrooms and flour, and stir well so that the flour amalgamates with the mushroom juices. Stir in the tomato purée and gradually add the stock. Add the tomatoes and sweetcorn. Season to taste with salt and pepper, bring to the boil and pour over the chicken in the casserole.

Cover the casserole and cook in a preheated oven, gas mark 3 (160°C, 325°F), for one hour. Skim off any fat, sprinkle with the parsley and serve.

Serves 4
Fat content per serving 16 g
Energy content per serving 388 kilocalories

VEGETABLE AND BEAN RISOTTO

1 teaspoon mono-unsaturated or polyunsaturated oil
1 large onion, sliced
2 leeks, cleaned and thinly sliced
2 sticks celery, chopped
1 clove garlic, crushed
8 oz (225 g) rice
4 oz (100 g) mushrooms, chopped
1 × 8-oz (225-g) can red kidney beans, drained
1 × 8-oz (225-g) can tomatoes
1 pint (600 ml) vegetable stock
salt and black pepper

Heat the oil in a large heavy-bottomed saucepan and gently cook the onion until soft. Add the leeks and celery and cook for a further two minutes, then add the garlic, rice, mushrooms and beans. Cook for another two minutes, stirring continuously, then add the tomatoes and their juice, and the stock. Bring to the boil and add salt and pepper to taste. Cover and simmer for 30–40 minutes until the rice is tender, adding more stock if the rice looks dry during cooking.

Serves 4
Fat content per serving 4 g
Energy content per serving 316 kilocalories

SPICY VEGETABLE STEW

8 oz (225 g) potatoes, cubed
1 tablespoon mono-unsaturated or polyunsaturated oil
1 onion, chopped
1 clove garlic, crushed
1 pinch turmeric

1 teaspoon ground coriander
1 teaspoon ground cumin
1 pinch chilli powder
1 pinch garam masala
1 × 8-oz (225-g) can tomatoes
1 × 14-oz (400-g) can chickpeas, drained and rinsed
$\frac{1}{2}$ pint (300 ml) vegetable stock
juice of 1 lemon
salt and black pepper
1 tablespoon freshly chopped parsley

Cook the potatoes in boiling water until soft. Drain and set aside.

Heat the oil in a large saucepan and cook the onion gently until it is soft. Add the garlic and all the spices, with the exception of the garam masala, and cook for a further three minutes. Add the tomatoes and their juices and cook for a further five minutes over a gentle heat. Add the chickpeas, potatoes, stock, lemon juice and seasoning, bring to the boil and simmer for 20 minutes. Sprinkle with garam masala and parsley, and serve.

Serves 4
Fat content per serving 8 g
Energy content per serving 243 kilocalories

MACARONI, TOMATO AND MUSHROOM BAKE

8 oz (225 g) wholewheat macaroni
2 teaspoons olive oil
1 onion, chopped
4 oz (100 g) mushrooms, sliced
1 clove garlic, crushed
1 × 14-oz (400-g) can tomatoes
4 tablespoons tomato purée
2 tablespoons freshly chopped thyme
salt and freshly milled black pepper
2 oz (50 g) low-fat hard cheese, grated
1 tablespoon freshly chopped parsley, to garnish

Cook the macaroni in boiling water for 15–20 minutes until *al dente*, drain, refresh under cold water, drain thoroughly and toss in one teaspoon of olive oil. Set to one side.

Heat the remaining oil in a large saucepan and cook the onion gently until soft. Add the mushrooms and garlic, cook for a further five minutes then add the tomatoes, the tomato purée, the thyme and seasoning. Bring to the boil and add the cooked macaroni. Make certain it is heated right through, then pour into an ovenproof dish, top with the cheese and place under a preheated grill until the top is browned. Sprinkle with chopped parsley to serve.

Serves 4
Fat content per serving 6 g
Energy content per serving 270 kilocalories

VEGETABLE CURRY

> 1 tablespoon mono-unsaturated or polyunsaturated oil
> 2 onions, sliced
> 2 cloves garlic, crushed
> 1/2 teaspoon turmeric
> 1/2 teaspoon ground cumin
> 1/2 teaspoon ground coriander
> 1/2 teaspoon ground ginger
> 1 teaspoon garam masala
> 1/2 teaspoon chilli powder
> 12 oz (350 g) potatoes, diced
> 4 oz (100 g) carrots, sliced
> 2 tablespoons tomato purée
> 3/4 pint (450 ml) vegetable stock
> 4 oz (100 g) fresh peas, shelled or frozen peas
> 1 cauliflower, chopped into florets
> 1 × 8-oz (225-g) can butter beans, drained and rinsed

Heat the oil in a large saucepan and cook the onion gently until soft and golden. Add the garlic and all the spices and cook for a further three to five minutes. Add the potatoes, carrots, tomato purée and stock, bring to the boil and simmer for 15 minutes. Add the peas, cauliflower and butter beans, bring back to the boil and simmer until the cauliflower florets are just tender. Serve hot.

Serves 6
Fat content per serving 3 g
Energy content per serving 150 kilocalories

BEEF CURRY

> *1 teaspoon mono-unsaturated or polyunsaturated oil*
> *1 lb (450 g) very lean beef, all visible fat removed, cubed*
> *2 onions, chopped*
> *2 cloves garlic, crushed*
> *1 teaspoon curry powder*
> *½ teaspoon ground mixed spice*
> *½ teaspoon garam masala*
> *2 tablespoons tomato purée*
> *1 × 14-oz (400-g) can tomatoes*
> *4 oz (100 g) dried apricots, chopped*
> *2 oz (50 g) raisins*
> *1 pint (600 ml) beef or vegetable stock*
> *1–2 tablespoons cornflour*

In a heavy-bottomed saucepan heat the oil and cook the beef cubes until they are browned. Add the onions and continue to cook until they are soft and golden. Add the garlic and spices and cook for a further five minutes, then stir in the tomato purée, tomatoes, dried fruit and stock. Slowly bring to the boil, cover and simmer for one hour.

Mix the cornflour with a little cold water to make a thin paste. Stirring all the while, slowly add the liquid to the curry until it has thickened to the right consistency. Allow to stand for 10–20 minutes and serve with rice.

Serves 6
Fat content per serving 5 g
Energy content per serving 183 kilocalories

PORK AND APPLE CASSEROLE

*1 lb (450 g) very lean pork, all visible fat removed,
    diced*
6 oz (150 g) lean back bacon, all visible fat removed
2 onions, chopped
2 green dessert apples, cored and sliced
salt and black pepper
¾ lb (350 g) potatoes, sliced
½ pint (300 ml) chicken or vegetable stock
2 tablespoons freshly chopped parsley, to garnish

Place the pork in the base of an ovenproof casserole. Grill
the bacon and drain off any fat. Chop the bacon and place
it in the casserole with the pork. Add the onions, apples
and seasoning and top with a layer of potatoes. Pour over
the stock and, if necessary, top up with water until the
liquid just comes up to the layer of potatoes. Cover and
bake in a preheated oven, gas mark 4 (180°C, 350°F), for
one hour. Remove the casserole lid and bake for a further
15 minutes to brown the potatoes.

  Skim off any excess fat, and serve with chopped parsley
sprinkled on top.

Serves 6
Fat content per serving 8 g
Energy content per serving 233 kilocalories

STEWED BEEF WITH VEGETABLES AND
LENTILS

3 tablespoons water
*1½ lb (750 g) very lean beef, all visible fat removed,
    cubed*
4 oz (100 g) carrots, diced
1 onion, roughly chopped
4 oz (100 g) red lentils
2 tablespoons wholemeal flour
salt and black pepper
2 tablespoons tomato purée

100

1 pint (600 ml) beef stock
2 tablespoons chopped parsley, to garnish

Pour the water into a large saucepan, bring to the boil, add the meat and cook until it has taken colour. Add the carrots and onions and cook until they have softened. Add the lentils, flour and seasoning and stir until the flour has absorbed all the liquid. Stir in the tomato purée. Slowly pour in the stock, bring to the boil, mix well and transfer to an ovenproof casserole. Cook, covered, in a preheated oven, gas mark 3 (160°C, 325°F), for one hour, by which time the meat should be tender. Skim off any excess fat and serve topped with parsley.

Serves 6
Fat content per serving 6 g
Energy content per serving 234 kilocalories

LAMB AND VEGETABLE CASSEROLE

2 teaspoons mono-unsaturated or polyunsaturated oil
1½ lb (750 g) very lean lamb, all visible fat removed, diced
4 oz (100 g) carrots, sliced
1 turnip, diced
1 onion, chopped
½ teaspoon freshly chopped rosemary
1–2 tablespoons wholemeal flour
1 tablespoon tomato purée
¾ pint (450 ml) meat or vegetable stock
salt and black pepper
small sprig fresh rosemary

Heat the oil in a large saucepan over moderate heat and fry the lamb until it is brown all over. Add the vegetables and chopped rosemary and cook, stirring, until they have browned. Sprinkle over the flour and stir until all the meat and vegetables are coated. Add the tomato purée, stock and seasoning, bring to the boil and transfer to a casserole. Cook in a preheated oven, gas mark 4 (180°C, 350°F) for about one hour. Allow to stand for 10–15 minutes, skim off any fat, and serve.

Alternatively leave to cool overnight, take off any solidified fat with a spatula, then reheat the casserole before serving.

Serve garnished with a sprig of fresh rosemary.

Serves 6
Fat content per serving 13 g
Energy content per serving 265 kilocalories

PUDDINGS AND DESSERTS

APRICOT AND ALMOND RICE PUDDING

Many people add jam to rice pudding when they are eating it. This recipe comes with its own fruit.

> *1 pint (600 ml) skimmed milk*
> *3–4 oz (75–100 g) short-grain rice pudding*
> *2 oz (50 g) caster sugar*
> *2 oz (50 g) dried apricots, chopped*
> *1 oz (25 g) flaked almonds*
> *½ teaspoon grated nutmeg*

Place the milk into a saucepan, add the rice and sugar and bring to the boil. Reduce the heat and summer for two minutes.

Sprinkle the chopped apricots and the flaked almonds in a lightly greased ovenproof dish. Pour over the milk, rice and sugar mixture and sprinkle the nutmeg on top. Bake in a preheated oven, gas mark 3 (160°C, 325°F), for two hours.

Serves 4
Fat content per serving 4 g
Energy content per serving 223 kilocalories

SUMMER PUDDING

This is a delicious way of using up a glut of summer fruit –
the proportions and varieties of fruit can be varied,
depending on what's available.

> *12 oz (350 g) raspberries*
> *4 oz (100 g) black currants*
> *4 oz (100 g) red currants*
> *4 oz (100 g) granulated sugar*
> *4–6 slices stale brown or white bread, crusts removed*

Adding no water whatsoever, gently stew the fruit and
sugar in a saucepan for three to four minutes. Set aside to
cool.

Line a pudding bowl with some of the bread so that
there are no gaps between the slices. Spoon in the fruit,
reserving some of the juice. Cover the fruit with a
complete layer of sliced bread, place a tight-fitting plate
on top to act as a lid, and put a weight on top of the plate
so that the pudding is compressed. Leave to stand overnight in the fridge.

To serve, carefully turn the pudding out on to a serving
dish and pour over the remaining juice.

Serves 4
Fat content per serving 1 g
Energy content per serving 251 kilocalories

LEMON SORBET

> *grated rind and juice of 2 lemons*
> *6 fl oz (175 ml) chilled water*
> *1 tablespoon caster sugar*
> *1 egg white*

Combine the lemon rind and juice in a bowl with the water
and the sugar. Mix well. Pour into a plastic box and put in
the freezer. When ice particles are just beginning to form,
beat the egg white in a bowl until it is stiff, beat the
freezing lemon mixture to a smooth consistency and care-

fully fold in the egg white. Return the mixture to the freezer and allow to freeze hard. Before serving allow it to soften slightly by transferring it to the refrigerator for one to two hours.

Serves 4
Fat content per serving – none
Energy content per serving 19 kilocalories

STRAWBERRY SORBET
Sorbets can very easily be made from most soft fruits; strawberries are used here, but you could just as easily use raspberries, black currants or blackberries.

> *8 oz (225 g) caster sugar*
> *1 pint (600 ml) water*
> *1 lb (450 g) hulled strawberries*
> *2 teaspoons lemon juice*
> *4 egg whites*

Make up a syrup by heating the sugar and water together in a saucepan over a low heat, stirring constantly until the sugar has dissolved. Simmer for 10 minutes, then remove from the heat and allow to cool.

Place the fruit in a saucepan with a little water and simmer until the fruit has softened. Rub the fruit through a sieve to make a purée. Stir the purée into the sugar syrup and make it up to two pints (1.2 litres) with extra water. When the mixture is cool, add the lemon juice and pour into a shallow flat container. Freeze until nearly firm.

Whisk the egg whites until lightly stiff. Scrape the frozen mixture out of its container and put into a cooled bowl. Break it up with a fork and fold in the egg whites. Return the mixture to the container and freeze until firm.

Serves 6
Fat content per serving – none
Energy content per serving 174 kilocalories

LOW-FAT CHRISTMAS PUDDING

This just goes to show that anything is possible. Unlike an ordinary Christmas pudding, however, this will not keep well, and should be made in the week prior to Christmas.

1 lb (450 g) wholemeal breadcrumbs
8 oz (225 g) currants
8 oz (225 g) sultanas
4 oz (100 g) cored and grated apple
4 oz (100 g) peeled bananas, chopped
4 oz (100 g) Brazil nuts, chopped
8 oz (225 g) dark brown sugar
juice and rind of 1 lemon
1 tablespoon mixed spice
1 oz (25 g) chopped almonds
3 eggs
1/2 pint (300 ml) skimmed milk
1 teaspoon salt

In a large mixing bowl mix together all the ingredients and stir well. Spoon into a 4-pint (2.25 litre) pudding bowl or two 2-pint (1.25 litre) pudding bowls and cover securely with greaseproof paper, tied in place round the rim of the bowl.

Steam for three hours, topping up with boiling water as necessary. Allow to cool. Store in a cool dry place until Christmas Day and then steam for one hour before serving.

Serves 8
Fat content per serving 13 g
Energy content per serving 523 kilocalories

WINTER FRUIT SALAD

The dried fruits listed here are merely suggestions – use other varieties if you prefer.

3 oz (75 g) dried prunes
3 oz (75 g) dried apple rings
3 oz (75 g) dried apricots

3 oz (75 g) dried figs
3 oz (75 g) dried dates
juice and grated rind of 1 lemon
½ pint (300 ml) apple juice or
¼ pint (150 ml) apple juice and ¼ pint (150 ml)
sherry
4 tablespoons plain virtually fat-free fromage frais
4 oz (100 g) chopped toasted hazelnuts

Roughly chop all the dried fruit, removing the stones if necessary. Put them in a bowl with the lemon juice, lemon rind, apple juice (and sherry, if used). Cover, and leave to soak overnight.

The next day, transfer the contents of the bowl to a saucepan and simmer over a low heat until the fruits are soft. Allow to cool and divide into four bowls. Top with fromage frais and decorate with the chopped nuts.

Serves 4
Fat content per serving 10 g
Energy content per serving 383 kilocalories

BREAD AND MILK PUDDING

12 oz (350 g) wholemeal sliced bread
4 oz (100 g) dried fruit – sultanas, currants, etc.
2 eggs
1 oz (25 g) granulated sugar
1 teaspoon mixed spice
1 pint (600 ml) skimmed milk

In a greased ovenproof dish layer the sliced bread with the dried fruit, starting and ending with bread.

Beat the eggs in a mixing bowl. Stir in the sugar, mixed spice and milk. Pour this mixture carefully over the bread. Bake in a preheated oven, gas mark 4 (180°C, 350°F), for about 40 minutes, or until the pudding is set and the top lightly browned.

Serves 4

Fat content per serving 6 g
Energy content per serving 363 kilocalories

PANCAKES
We have included pancakes with desserts as, traditionally, they have been served as a pudding with lemon juice and sugar, on Shrove Tuesday. However, as a dessert, you can serve them with all sorts of fruit and stewed fruit fillings, and as a savoury dish with innumerable different savoury stuffings, fillings and sauces.

> *4 oz (100 g) plain flour*
> *pinch of salt*
> *1 egg*
> *½ pint skimmed milk*

Sift the flour and salt into a bowl. Beat the egg in a separate bowl and pour it into a well in the centre of the flour. Add half the milk, work the flour into the milk and egg and then whisk until all the lumps have disappeared. Allow to stand for 10–15 minutes, then add the rest of the milk and whisk again.

To cook the pancakes you need a clean frying pan or omelette pan. Wipe the surface of the pan with kitchen paper soaked in mono-unsaturated or polyunsaturated oil, heat the pan until it is very hot, then pour over just enough batter to cover the base. Cook for one minute. Turn the pancake over with a spatula and cook the other side for one minute. Turn the pancake out on to a warm plate, fold it in half then in half again, and keep warm until all the pancakes are cooked. Serve immediately, unless they are to be stuffed and cooked further.

Makes 8–10 pancakes
Fat content per pancake 1 g
Energy content per pancake 66 kilocalories

DRIED FRUIT HOT POT

1 lb (450g) dried fruit, e.g. apricots, figs, apples, pears, pitted prunes
3 pints (1.75 litres) lapsang souchong or keemun tea, strained
½ lemon, sliced
2 bay leaves
1 teaspoon grated nutmeg
2 oz (50g) cashew nuts
2 oz (50g) hazelnuts
2 oz (50g) walnut halves
2 oz (50g) almonds

Put all the dried fruit in a casserole, pour on the tea and leave to stand overnight. Add the lemon slices, bay leaves and nutmeg, cover and bake in a preheated oven, gas mark 4 (180°C, 350°F), for 1½ hours. Remove from the oven and, while it is cooling, toast or dry-fry the nuts until they are crisp but not burnt. Stir the toasted nuts into the warm fruit before serving.

Serves 6
Fat content per serving 16 g
Energy content per serving 330 kilocalories

9

SPECIAL OCCASIONS

SOUPS

LETTUCE SOUP

This soup is a delicious way of using up a glut of lettuces from the garden, or some lettuce in the refrigerator that is too limp for a salad.

> $^1/_2$ teaspoon mono-unsaturated or polyunsaturated oil
> 1 onion, chopped
> 8–12 oz (225–350 g) lettuce leaves, washed and chopped
> $^1/_2$ pint (300 ml) chicken stock
> $^1/_4$ pint (150 ml) white wine
> 2 teaspoons honey
> grated nutmeg, to taste
> milled black pepper, to taste
> $^1/_2$ pint (300 ml) skimmed milk
> 4 oz (100 g) plain virtually fat-free yoghurt
> 1 tablespoon freshly chopped mint, to garnish

In a large saucepan heat the oil, add the onion and fry gently until it is soft and golden. Add the chopped lettuce leaves, stock, wine, honey, nutmeg and pepper and bring to the boil. Reduce the heat and simmer for five to 10 minutes, until the lettuce is soft. Remove from the heat and allow to cool. Liquidise in a blender or food processor and set to one side.

In a bowl mix together the milk and the yoghurt. Add to the soup in a clean saucepan and gently heat the liquid through. Serve sprinkled with chopped mint.

Serves 4
Fat content per serving 2 g
Energy content per serving 100 kilocalories

CARROT SOUP

1/2 teaspoon mono-unsaturated or polyunsaturated oil
1 small onion, chopped
1 leek, chopped
1 small potato, peeled and chopped
1 lb (450 g) carrots, scrubbed and chopped
2 pints (1.2 litres) vegetable or chicken stock
salt and pepper to taste
4 oz (100 g) virtually fat-free yoghurt
1 tablespoon freshly chopped parsley or chervil, to garnish

Heat the oil in a saucepan, add the chopped onion and leek and fry gently until the onion is soft and golden; do not allow it to burn at all. Add the chopped potato and carrots, cook for a further two to three minutes, then add the stock and season to taste. Bring to the boil, reduce the heat and simmer for 15 minutes.

Allow the soup to cool. Liquidise in a food mill, blender or processor and return the soup to a clean saucepan. Reheat gently and pour into bowls. Swirl some yoghurt into each bowl, and sprinkle over the chopped herbs.

Serves 4
Fat content per serving 1 g
Energy content per serving 100 kilocalories

WATERCRESS SOUP

>*2 bunches of watercress*
>*$1/2$ teaspoon mono-unsaturated or polyunsaturated oil*
>*1 large onion*
>*10 oz (350 g) potatoes, peeled and sliced*
>*1 pint (600 ml) chicken or vegetable stock*
>*1 bay leaf*
>*$1/2$ teaspoon grated nutmeg*
>*salt and freshly milled black pepper*
>*$1/2$ pint (300 ml) skimmed milk*
>*2 tablespoons virtually fat-free plain fromage frais*

Carefully wash the watercress, discarding any coarse stalks and yellow leaves, and chop coarsely.

Heat the oil in a heavy-bottomed saucepan, and cook the onion and watercress over gentle heat for five to seven minutes. Add the potatoes, stock, bay leaf and nutmeg and bring to the boil. Reduce the heat and simmer until the potatoes are soft.

Remove the pan from the heat and liquidise the soup in a blender or food processor. Return to a clean pan and heat through gently. Add the milk, season to taste and continue to cook, stirring, until hot. Divide between six soup bowls. To each one add a teaspoon of fromage frais, and serve immediately.

Serves 6
Fat content per serving 0.6 g
Energy content per serving 85 kilocalories

STARTERS

TOMATO SORBET
This is a variation on a fruit sorbet, and makes a very refreshing beginning to a summer meal.

>*3 lb (1.5 kg) tomatoes, chopped*
>*1 onion, chopped*

1 tablespoon freshly chopped basil or marjoram
1 tablespoon tomato purée
juice of 1 lemon
salt and freshly ground black pepper
honey to taste
sprigs of fresh applemint

Put the tomatoes, onion and basil or marjoram into a heavy-bottomed saucepan set over a moderate heat. Bring to the boil and simmer for 30 minutes, stirring occasionally. Rub through a sieve into a bowl, to liquidise the mixture and to remove the pips, then stir in the tomato purée, lemon juice, seasoning and honey. Leave the mixture to cool, pour into a plastic box and freeze overnight.

An hour before serving, transfer the box to the refrigerator. Just before serving, place the frozen mixture in a large bowl and break it up, crushing it, with a rolling pin. Divide the crushed sorbet between six individual bowls, garnish with a sprig of mint and serve.

Serves 6
Fat content per serving – none
Energy content per serving 27 kilocalories

SOUSED HERRINGS

6 small herrings
¹/₂ pint (300 ml) white wine vinegar
¹/₂ pint (300 ml) water
6 juniper berries
6 cloves
2 bay leaves
6 peppercorns
6 teaspoons German mustard
6 pickled gherkins
2 onions, sliced into thin rings

Gut and clean the herrings, removing the heads, open them out and remove the bones. Pat the fillets dry and put to one side.

Put the vinegar, water, juniper berries, cloves, bay leaves and peppercorns into a saucepan, bring to the boil and simmer for 10 minutes. Put to one side.

Spread mustard on the inside of each opened-out herring. Place a gherkin at the head end of each herring, some small onion rings down the inside, and roll each herring up from the head to the tail, securing each with a cocktail stick through the middle. Place the rolled-up herrings in an ovenproof dish, pour over the marinade, sprinkle with the remaining onion rings and cover. Bake in a preheated oven, gas mark 4 (180°C, 350°F), for 15–20 minutes. Allow to cool. Store in the refrigerator for one to two days before serving.

Serves 6
Fat content per serving 28 g
Energy content per serving 383 kilocalories

CAULIFLOWER AND PRAWN BOMBE
The prawns nestling in the cauliflower head provide quite a surprise. This makes a very pretty summer starter.

1 medium cauliflower
8 oz (225 g) cooked peeled prawns
6 tablespoons plain virtually fat-free fromage frais
2 tablespoons plain virtually fat-free yoghurt
1 bunch chives, chopped
freshly milled black pepper

Remove all the leaves from the cauliflower and slice across the bottom to remove the base of the stalk and perhaps the bottoms of the lower florets; the aim is to allow the cauliflower to stand on a flat surface.

Boil the cauliflower in a little salted water so that it part boils, part steams. Remove it from the heat before it gets soft, take it out of the saucepan and allow it to drain and to get completely cold.

Place the cold cauliflower on a serving plate and push the prawns in between the florets, spacing them evenly. In

113

a bowl, mix together the fromage frais, the yoghurt and the chopped chives, and spoon over the cauliflower. Grind pepper over it and serve immediately.

Serves 4
Fat content per serving 2g
Energy content per serving 105 kilocalories

Mussels

Visitors to France may well have had mussels, usually in the classic dish *moules marinière*. In contrast, mussels are rarely served in this country, despite the fact that they are easy to cook.

Allow about 1 pint (600ml) mussels per person. If they have not been cleaned you must throw away any broken or open specimens and any that are not sealed tight shut; then scrape off the seaweedy-looking 'beard' and any barnacles. Scrub the shells and wash in several rinses of cold water.

The simplest method of cooking mussels is to place them in a large saucepan, sprinkle with salt (one teaspoon per serving), heat the pan until the mussels start to open and the juices begin to run. Remove from the heat, transfer the mussels to a warm bowl, pour over the juices and serve.

Here is a slightly more ambitious method, cooking them in wine.

MUSSELS IN WHITE WINE

> *4 pints (2.25 litres) mussels, cleaned and washed*
> *8 fl oz (250ml) dry white wine*
> *2 cloves garlic, crushed*
> *freshly milled black pepper*
> *2 tablespoons freshly chopped parsley*

Put the mussels in a large saucepan. Add the wine, garlic and pepper. Set the pan over moderately high heat and shake it gently with the lid on until the mussels open. Remove the mussels to a warm bowl. Add the chopped

114

parsley to the liquid remaining in the pan and pour it over the mussels. Serve immediately with fresh rolls or French bread to mop up the sauce.

Serves 4
Fat content per serving 4g
Energy content per serving 174 kilocalories

Finally a note about eating mussels. You can use a fork to fish them out of their shells, or your fingers, but neither are very satisfactory. The neatest method is to take the first one out of its shell with your fingers, and then use the empty shells as 'tongs' to extract all the remaining mussels and pop them into your mouth.

FRUITY FISH KEBABS

finely grated rind of 1 orange
finely grated rind of 1 lemon
juice of 1 lemon
juice of 1 grapefruit
2 cloves garlic, crushed
2 tablespoons demerara sugar
freshly milled black pepper
3 tablespoons olive oil
1½lb (750g) monkfish, cut into 1-inch (2.5-cm) cubes
1 red pepper, cored, deseeded and cut into rectangles
1 yellow pepper, cored, deseeded and cut into rectangles
4 slices each of lemon, orange and grapefruit, to garnish

Mix the orange and lemon rind with the lemon and grapefruit juice, garlic, sugar, black pepper and olive oil. Put the cubed fish into a glass or porcelain dish, pour over the marinade, cover and stand in the refrigerator overnight.

Thread pieces of fish, pepper and fruit, fish, pepper, fruit, and so on, on to kebab skewers. Place the skewers on a grill rack under a preheated grill, or over a barbecue,

115

and cook for about five to six minutes, brushing two or three times with the remaining marinade, and turning once. Serve garnished with slices of citrus fruit.

Serves 6
Fat content per serving 9 g
Energy content per serving 194 kilocalories

Crudités

Crudités are slices of raw vegetables that are eaten with various dips. Here are some ideas for vegetables with some low-fat dips to accompany them.

SUITABLE VEGETABLES

> *Use fresh, well-washed raw vegetables, e.g. carrot, turnip, cucumber, courgette, celery, mushrooms, cauliflower, broccoli, spring onion, sliced into strips or broken into pieces*
> *wholewheat grissini (bread sticks)*

Allow 4–6 oz (100–150 g) vegetables per person. Place the dips in the centre of the table, and allow each person to help themselves to raw vegetables which they then dunk in the dips before eating.

Fat content per serving of vegetables – trace
Energy content per serving of vegetables 14 kilocalories

AUBERGINE SAUCE

> *2 teaspoons olive oil*
> *1 small aubergine, chopped*
> *1 red pepper, cored, deseeded and chopped*
> *1 onion, chopped*
> *1 stick celery, finely chopped*
> *2 cloves garlic, crushed*
> *1 tablespoon tomato purée*
> *4 fl oz (120 ml) water*
> *1 tablespoon red wine vinegar*
> *1 tablespoon drained capers*

2 teaspoons brown sugar
2 tablespoons freshly chopped basil or parsley
4 oz (100 g) black olives, stoned and chopped

Heat the oil in a saucepan and cook the chopped aubergine for about 10–15 minutes until it is soft and has
browned, but do not let it burn. Add the pepper, onion,
celery and garlic and cook until the onion is soft. Stir in
the tomato purée, water, vinegar, capers, sugar, basil or
parsley and olives. Increase the heat and cook for another
10–15 minutes or until the sauce has thickened, stirring
constantly. Allow to cool. Transfer to a blender or food
processor and work to a purée. Serve chilled or at room
temperature.

Serves 8
Fat content per serving 4 g
Energy content per serving 58 kilocalories

SPINACH DIP

12 oz (350 g) young spinach leaves, cooked and finely
*   chopped*
3 spring onions, finely chopped
2 tablespoons freshly chopped parsley or coriander
1 tablespoon lemon juice
4 fl oz (120 ml) plain virtually fat-free yoghurt
4 oz (100 g) very-low-fat soft cheese
1 teaspoon freshly ground black pepper
pinch of salt
2 cloves garlic, crushed

Squeeze out as much liquid from the chopped cooked
spinach leaves as possible. Place the spinach in a blender
or food processor with the remaining ingredients and work
to a purée. Served chilled.

Serves 8
Fat content per serving 1 g
Energy content per serving 36 kilocalories

AVOCADO DIP

2 large ripe avocados
juice of 1 lemon
8 oz (225 g) very-low-fat cream cheese or curd cheese
4 tomatoes, peeled, blanched, liquidised and sieved
2 large cloves garlic, crushed
1 onion, finely chopped
salt and freshly milled black pepper
1 tablespoon freshly chopped parsley

Halve each avocado, remove the stones and scoop out the flesh into a mixing bowl. Mash well until smooth and stir in the lemon juice. In a separate bowl mash the cheese, tomatoes, garlic, onion, seasoning and parsley until well blended. Combine this evenly with the avocado mixture. Cover and refrigerate until chilled. If liked, serve in the avocado shells.

Serves 8
Fat content per serving 21 g
Energy content per serving 257 kilocalories

SMOKED MACKEREL PÂTÉ

2 smoked mackerel fillets, skinned
8 oz (225 g) very-low-fat curd cheese
1 tablespoon horseradish sauce
juice of 1/2 lemon
freshly ground black pepper
4 oz (100 g) smoked salmon in thin sheets
sprigs of flat-leaf parsley

Chop the smoked mackerel into small pieces and shred the flesh with two forks. Place the fish in a bowl and beat in the curd cheese, horseradish sauce, lemon juice and pepper.

Line the base of a suitably sized bowl with half the smoked salmon. Spoon in the smoked mackerel mixture, press it down and smooth the top. Cover with the

118

remaining smoked salmon. Refrigerate for a minimum of four hours and preferably overnight. Turn out on to a round flat serving plate and garnish with the sprigs of parsley.

Serves 4
Fat content per serving 23 g
Energy content per serving 355 kilocalories

STUFFED MUSHROOMS ·

> *8 large mushrooms, wiped clean*
> *¹/₂ teaspoon mono-unsaturated or polyunsaturated oil*
> *1 onion, chopped*
> *4 sticks celery, finely chopped*
> *1 teaspoon freshly chopped thyme*
> *1 teaspoon freshly chopped parsley*
> *2 cloves garlic, crushed*
> *3 oz (75 g) chopped walnuts*
> *4 oz (100 g) very-low-fat curd cheese*
> *1 egg*

Remove the stalks from the mushrooms, chop the stalks finely and set to one side.

To make the stuffing, heat the oil in a saucepan and cook the onion gently until soft, then add the celery, mushroom stalks, herbs and garlic. Stir well and simmer for 10 minutes. Stir in 2 oz (50 g) walnuts and continue to cook, stirring, for a further five minutes.

In a bowl mix the curd cheese with the egg. Add the mushroom, onion and celery mixture, stir well and spoon into the mushroom caps. Sprinkle with the remaining chopped walnuts and place on a lightly oiled baking sheet. Bake in a preheated oven, gas mark 4 (180°C, 350°F), for 30 minutes. Serve immediately.

Serves 4
Fat content per serving 14 g
Energy content per serving 172 kilocalories

MAIN COURSES

PIGEON BREASTS WITH APRICOTS

Pigeons are now widely available in butchers' shops and even in some supermarkets. It is a dark meat, but with very little fat, and what fat there is is low in saturates. Although straightforward to cook, they can be a little fiddly to eat, with lots of small bones; this recipe therefore uses pigeon breasts, but if you cannot obtain these use whole pigeons cut in half.

> *1 large onion, sliced*
> *1 teaspoon olive oil*
> *1 lb (450 g) pigeon breasts or 2 pigeons, halved*
> *8 oz (225 g) chickpeas, soaked overnight*
> *1 teaspoon ground cinnamon*
> *salt and pepper to taste*
> *8 oz (225 g) dried apricots, pre-soaked until soft*
> *1 teaspoon lemon juice*
> *1 tablespoon freshly chopped coriander, parsley or lovage*

In a frying pan or cast iron casserole, heat the oil and fry the onion gently until golden. Add the pigeon breasts or halved pigeons and brown them all over. If cooked in a frying pan, transfer to a casserole and add the chickpeas, cinnamon, salt and pepper, and cover with boiling water. Cook in a preheated oven, gas mark 5 (190°C, 375°F), for one hour, or until the pigeon meat and chickpeas are soft.

Add the apricots and cook for another 20 minutes. Remove from the oven and add the lemon juice. Adjust the seasoning if necessary.

Serve with couscous (see page 143) and garnish with chopped herbs.

Serves 4
Fat content per serving 23 g
Energy content per serving 507 kilocalories

PHEASANT AND APPLE

This is an old Hampshire recipe, modified by the substitution of yoghurt for cream. Watercress, which is widely grown in the county, is important as it counterbalances the sweetness of the apples.

> 2–3 teaspoons mono-unsaturated or polyunsaturated oil
> 2 young pheasants
> 10 cooking apples, peeled, cored and sliced
> 2–3 bay leaves
> 2 oz (50 g) muscovado sugar
> 4 oz (100 g) plain virtually fat-free yoghurt
> salt and freshly milled pepper to taste
> 2 oz (50 g) toasted wholemeal breadcrumbs
> 4 tablespoons chopped watercress

Heat the oil in a large frying pan or saucepan, then brown each pheasant in turn. Set pheasants and juices to one side.

Arrange the apple slices and the bay leaves in the bottom of a casserole. Sprinkle on the sugar and place the two pheasants on top. Pour over first the juices from browning the pheasants then the yoghurt. Season, cover and cook in a preheated oven, gas mark 4 (180°C, 350°F), for 1–1½ hours.

Before serving, sprinkle over the breadcrumbs and the chopped watercress.

Serves 6
Fat content per serving 24 g
Energy content per serving 700 kilocalories

CHICKEN BREASTS WITH SPRING ONIONS

> 4 oz (100 g) spring onions, trimmed and chopped
> 2 teaspoons fresh root ginger, peeled and chopped
> 2 teaspoons chopped garlic
> pared rind and juice of 1 lemon
> salt and freshly milled black pepper

4 chicken breasts, skinned and boned
14 fl oz (400 ml) chicken stock

Mix 3 oz (75 g) of the spring onions in a shallow glass or porcelain dish with the ginger, garlic and lemon rind. Season with salt and pepper. Add the chicken breasts, cover and leave to stand in the refrigerator for at least 12 hours and preferably 24 hours, turning the meat several times.

Extract the lemon rind from the ingredients, blanch it in boiling water for three minutes and cut into fine strips. Scrape the remaining ingredients from the chicken, place them in a saucepan with the stock, bring to the boil, cover and simmer for 10 minutes. Strain the stock, pressing the ingredients with a spoon to extract all the liquid. Return the stock to a small pan and boil for 10–15 minutes to reduce it. Remove from the heat and stir in the remaining spring onions, the strips of lemon rind, and the lemon juice to taste. Season if necessary.

Grill the chicken breasts for about four to five minutes on each side – they should be cooked through, but still moist.

Warm the sauce gently. Cut the chicken breasts into ½-inch (1 cm) slices, crosswise on the diagonal, fan out on a serving plate and spoon the sauce around the meat.

Serves 4
Fat content per serving 8 g
Energy content per serving 300 kilocalories

FISH PARCELS

6 small herrings or mackerel, gutted and cleaned, heads removed
or 6 medium fish cutlets, cleaned
6 large rectangles of baking parchment or grease-proof paper
12 oz (350 g) button mushrooms, sliced
3 medium onions, thinly sliced
4 tomatoes, thinly sliced

12 oz (350 g) shelled peas or frozen peas
6 tablespoons tomato purée
pinch of dried oregano in each parcel
pinch of dried rosemary in each parcel
salt and freshly milled black pepper
2 tablespoons lemon juice
6 tablespoons dry white wine

Place each fish or piece of fish on a piece of baking parchment or greaseproof paper large enough to be folded over and tied together at the top. On top of each piece of fish strew the mushrooms, onions, tomatoes, peas and a tablespoon of tomato purée. Sprinkle lightly with herbs and season to taste. Gather up the paper, spoon in the lemon juice and wine and tie up the paper with string. Arrange the fish parcels on a baking tray. Cook in a preheated oven, gas mark 4 (180°C, 350°F), for 20–30 minutes until the fish is tender.

Serve the parcels complete, allowing each person to open their own.

Serves 6
Fat content per serving 33 g
Energy content per serving 536 kilocalories

HERBY STEAKS

4 very lean beef steaks, all visible fat trimmed off
2 cloves garlic, crushed
1 teaspoon freshly chopped rosemary
1 teaspoon freshly chopped thyme
juice of 1/2 lemon
salt and freshly milled black pepper
To garnish:
parsley sprigs
4 tomatoes, sliced

Beat out the steaks with a meat hammer or rolling pin and place them on a flat plate or dish. Mix the garlic, herbs, lemon juice and seasoning and spread over the steaks.

Cover the steaks with another plate, and leave in the refrigerator overnight.

Place the steaks under a preheated hot grill for two to seven minutes each side, depending on the degree of rareness preferred. Serve as soon as they are cooked, garnished with sprigs of parsley and sliced tomato.

Serves 4
Fat content per serving 9 g
Energy content per serving 267 kilocalories

VEGETABLE STUFFED AUBERGINES

2 large aubergines
1 onion, chopped
1 clove garlic, crushed
1 green pepper, cored, deseeded and chopped
1 red pepper, cored, deseeded and chopped
1 tablespoon olive oil
½ teaspoon chilli powder
1 × 8-oz (225 g) can tomatoes
salt and freshly milled black pepper
1 tablespoon chopped almonds
2 oz (50 g) low-fat hard cheese, grated
1 tablespoon freshly chopped parsley, to garnish

Slice the aubergines lengthwise. Remove the stalks and seeds. Scoop out the inside of the aubergines, taking care not to damage the skins. Chop the flesh and combine with the onion, garlic and peppers.

Heat most of the oil in a heavy-bottomed saucepan and gently cook the mixture until it is just soft. Add the chilli powder and cook for a further three minutes. Stir in the tomatoes and season to taste. Cook for five minutes over a moderate heat.

Divide the mixture between the four aubergine cases. With the remaining oil grease a large ovenproof dish. Pour in a little water, place the stuffed aubergine cases in the dish and sprinkle the almonds and cheese on top. Cook in a preheated oven, gas mark 4 (180°C, 350°F), until the aubergine cases are soft and the cheese and almond topping is golden brown. Serve hot, garnished with parsley.

Serves 4
Fat content per serving 15 g
Energy content per serving 198 kilocalories

BAKED NUT RISOTTO

1 teaspoon mono-unsaturated or polyunsaturated oil
1 onion, sliced
1 clove garlic, crushed
6 oz (175 g) long-grain brown rice
4 oz (100 g) mushrooms, sliced
1 oz (25 g) unsalted peanuts
1 oz (25 g) chopped walnuts
1 oz (25 g) hazelnuts
1½ pints (900 ml) vegetable stock
salt and freshly milled black pepper
2 oz (50 g) low-fat hard cheese, grated
1 tablespoon freshly chopped parsley, chives or coriander

Heat the oil in a large saucepan and add the onion and garlic. Cook gently until the onion is soft, then add the rice. Cook over a moderate heat until the rice starts to become clear in appearance. Add the mushrooms, nuts, stock and seasoning and bring to the boil.

Transfer the rice mixture to a casserole, cover and bake in a preheated oven, gas mark 3 (160°C, 325°F), for about 30 minutes. Remove from the oven and leave to stand for 15 minutes. Sprinkle with the grated cheese and return to a hot oven or place under a preheated grill for five minutes until the cheese has browned. Sprinkle with freshly chopped herbs and serve hot.

Serves 4
Fat content per serving 22 g
Energy content per serving 358 kilocalories

VEAL IN WINE AND TARRAGON SAUCE

There are two sorts of tarragon, French and Russian. Make sure you have French tarragon, as the Russian variety has next to no flavour.

> *1¼ lb (500g) lean boneless veal, all visible fat removed, cubed*
> *2 carrots, scrubbed and diced*
> *2 onions, sliced*
> *2 sticks celery, chopped*
> *1 bay leaf*
> *8 whole black peppercorns*
> *8 tablespoons dry white wine*
> *1 teaspoon cornflour*
> *8 oz (225g) button mushrooms*
> *salt and freshly milled black pepper*
> *½ teaspoon freshly chopped tarragon*
> *1 bunch watercress, washed and trimmed, to garnish*

Put the meat in a large saucepan, just cover with water, bring to the boil and skim. Add the carrots, onions, celery, bay leaf and peppercorns. Simmer for about one hour, by which time the meat should be tender. Strain the meat stock and allow to cool.

Put the meat and vegetables into a casserole and pour over the wine. Mix the cornflour with a little of the meat stock to make a thin paste and slowly blend it into the meat and wine mixture. Stir well, then add the mushrooms. Season to taste, add the tarragon and cook in a preheated oven, gas mark 4 (180°C, 350°F), for 15–30 minutes, until the sauce has thickened and the mushrooms are tender. Serve hot, garnished with watercress.

Serves 4
Fat content per serving 4g
Energy content per serving 200 kilocalories

126

PUDDINGS AND DESSERTS

BAKED COURGETTE PUDDING

2 tablespoons soft brown sugar
3 oz (75 g) sunflower margarine
1 oz (25 g) raisins
1 oz (25 g) currants
1 oz (25 g) chopped crystallised ginger
1 oz (25 g) uncoloured glacé cherries
2 teaspoons green ginger wine
1 tablespoon tepid water
6 oz (175 g) self-raising flour
8 oz (225 g) grated courgette
6 tablespoons virtually fat-free plain fromage frais

In a mixing bowl, beat together the margarine and sugar until light and fluffy, then mix in the dried fruit, crystallised ginger, cherries, ginger wine and water. Sift the flour on top, add the grated courgettes, then fold them in gently.

Spoon the mixture into six lightly greased individual ramekins and cook in a preheated oven, gas mark 4 (180°C, 350°F), for 15 minutes – they should feel springy to the touch. Serve immediately, with a tablespoon of fromage frais to top each one.

Serves 6
Fat content per serving 11 g
Energy content per serving 266 kilocalories

LIGHT LEMON CHEESECAKE

Base
    1½ oz (40 g) soya margarine
    4 oz (100 g) crushed oatcakes
Filling:
    1 × 12-oz (350-g) packet silken tofu
    5 oz (150 g) virtually fat-free plain yoghurt
    1 pkt lemon jelly

juice of 1 lemon
honey to taste
To decorate:
2 oz (50 g) white grapes, halved and seeded

Melt the margarine in a small pan. Stir in the oatcake crumbs. Press this mixture into an 8½-inch (22 cm) flan dish and refrigerate.

To make the filling, place the tofu and yoghurt in a blender or food processor and work to combine smoothly. Make up the jelly and allow the liquid to cool. Stir in the lemon juice and combine the jelly with the tofu and yoghurt mixture. Add a little honey, then pour the filling into the cooled base and refrigerate for a minimum of four hours, preferably overnight. Serve chilled, decorated with halved white grapes.

Serves 6
Fat content per serving 11 g
Energy content per serving 245 kilocalories

SUMMER FRUIT MERINGUE NESTS

Meringue
    3 egg whites
    6 oz (175 g) caster sugar
    a few drops of pink or red food colouring
    a few drops of almond essence
Filling
    6 oz (175 g) redcurrants
    6 oz (175 g) blackcurrants
    2 pears, peeled and chopped
    1 tablespoon caster sugar
    ¼ pint (150 ml) port
    8 oz (225 g) plain virtually fat-free fromage frais
    ½ oz (15 g) toasted flaked almonds, to decorate

To make the meringue, whisk the egg whites until they are stiff. Whisk in half the sugar then fold in the rest. Add a little colouring and flavouring – the mixture should have a

128

delicate colour and flavour. Spoon the meringue into a piping bag fitted with a star nozzle. Line two baking sheets with baking parchment. On to these pipe eight nests 3–4 inches (7.5–10 cm) in diameter. Bake the meringues in a cool oven, gas mark ¼ (110°C, 225°F), for two hours. Allow the meringues to cool in the oven.

To make the filling, place the fruit, sugar and port in a saucepan, cover and simmer gently for 10 minutes. Transfer to a bowl and allow the mixture to cool. Leave to stand, preferably in the refrigerator for at least six hours.

Fill the bottom of each meringue nest with fromage frais and spoon some of the fruit mixture on top. Sprinkle with toasted flaked almonds, and serve within two hours.

Serves 8
Fat content per serving 1 g
Energy content per serving 160 kilocalories

FRESH FRUIT OAT COCKTAIL

This can be served as a starter, but here it makes a delicious dessert. Any kind of fruit mixture can be used. Try pairs, plums and greengages; nectarines and peaches; strawberries, raspberries and red currants. For best results the hazelnuts should be skinned.

> *4 tablespoons porridge oats*
> *4 fl oz (100 ml) skimmed milk, warmed*
> *5 oz (150 g) plain virtually fat-free yoghurt*
> *4 tablespoons honey*
> *2 tablespoons lemon juice*
> *1 red apple, peeled, cored and grated*
> *1 green apple, peeled, cored and grated*
> *1 lb 2 oz (500 g) soft fruit, depending on the season*
> *4 tablespoons hazelnuts, toasted and chopped*
> *4 sprigs fresh mint*
> *4 raspberries or other items of soft fruit, to decorate*

Soak the oats in the warm milk for 15 minutes. Stir in the yoghurt, honey and lemon juice. Add the apples to the mixture, then cut up the soft fruit (if necessary) and fold in. Mix in the chopped nuts. Transfer to a serving bowl and decorate with sprigs of mint and whole raspberries. Serve chilled.

Serves 4
Fat content per serving 7 g
Energy content per serving 255 kilocalories

BAKED CARIBBEAN BANANAS

6 large ripe bananas
grated rind and juice of 2 lemons
4 oz (100 g) large raisins
4 oz (100 g) chopped walnuts
soft brown sugar or honey to taste
3 tablespoons rum
4 oz (100 g) plain virtually fat-free fromage frais
1 oz (25 g) flaked toasted almonds

Peel bananas, cut them lengthways and place them flat side downwards in an ovenproof dish. Sprinkle over the grated lemon rind and juice, the raisins, walnuts and sugar or honey. Add the rum and bake for 20–25 minutes in a preheated oven, gas mark 4 (180°C, 350°F), or until the fruit is just tender.

Serve hot, topped with fromage frais and almonds.

Serves 6
Fat content per serving 12 g
Energy content per serving 317 kilocalories

MIXED BERRY PUDDING

1½ lb (750 g) fresh or frozen raspberries and/or redcurrants
1½ lb (750 g) fresh or frozen blackberries and/or black currants
3 tablespoons ground rice
caster sugar or honey to taste
3 oz (75 g) plain virtually fat-free yoghurt
1 oz (25 g) toasted flaked almonds

Place the mixed soft fruit in a saucepan set over a gentle heat. Simmer until the fruit softens. Allow to cool, transfer to a blender or food processor and work to a purée.

Return the fruit purée to a clean saucepan and stir in the ground rice. Slowly bring the mixture to the boil and stir constantly until it thickens – about 20–25 minutes. Add sugar or honey to taste. Allow to cool and pour into six individual bowls.

Once the pudding has set, spread a thin layer of yoghurt over the top of each portion and strew with almonds.

Serves 6
Fat content per serving 3 g
Energy content per serving 157 kilocalories

STRAWBERRY FROZEN YOGHURT

10 oz (275 g) strawberries, hulled
4 oz (100 g) caster sugar
2 sachets gelatine
1 pint (600 ml) plain virtually fat-free yoghurt
2 tablespoons lemon juice
2 egg whites
To decorate:
whole strawberries
virtually fat-free plain fromage frais

Place the strawberries in a blender or food processor and work to a purée. Pour the purée into a bowl, sprinkle over 2 oz (50 g) of the sugar and leave to stand until you can pour off about four tablespoons of juice.

Pour the strawberry juice into a small saucepan and sprinkle the gelatine on top. Leave to stand for five minutes and then stir over a low heat until the gelatine has dissolved. Set aside and allow to cool.

In a bowl combine the yoghurt with the sweetened strawberry mixture and any remaining juice, the lemon juice and the gelatine and strawberry juice mixture. In a separate bowl beat the egg whites until they form soft peaks, then add the remaining 2 oz (50 g) sugar and beat until the mixture forms hard glossy peaks. Fold this meringue into the yoghurt mixture, pour into a plastic box and freeze until firm but still soft. It can be served like this, or frozen hard, in which case it should stand at room temperature for 30 minutes before serving.

Serve topped with a spoonful of fromage frais and a whole strawberry.

Serves 12–16
Fat content per serving 2 g
Energy content per serving 75 kilocalories

WHITE WINE ICE

8 fl oz (250 ml) water
6 oz caster sugar
12 fl oz (350 ml) medium dry white wine
12 fl oz (350 ml) white grape juice
1/4 pint (150 ml) freshly squeezed lemon juice
8 sprigs mint
4 oz (100 g) black grapes, seeded and halved

In a saucepan combine the water, sugar and wine. Bring to the boil, reduce the heat and simmer, uncovered, for five minutes. Allow the liquid to cool. Add the grape juice and lemon juice, transfer to a glass or porcelain container and chill. Pour the chilled liquid into ice cube trays and freeze.

When the cubes are frozen solid remove them from the tray and, working in batches, crush them in a blender or food processor until reduced to a slush. Pour the slush into a plastic box and re-freeze.

To serve, stand the ice at room temperature for about 30 minutes until it is soft enough to scoop into eight individual serving bowls. Decorate with mint leaves and halved grapes to serve.

Serves 8
Fat content per serving – none
Energy content per serving 152 kilocalories

BLACKCURRANT MOUSSE

1 lb (450 g) fresh or frozen black currants
1 small ripe banana, peeled and sliced
finely grated peel of 1 orange
1–2 tablespoons caster sugar
3 tablespoons water
3 teaspoons gelatine powder
1 egg white
1/2 pint (300 ml) very-low-fat black currant yoghurt

If using frozen black currants, defrost thoroughly before use. Reserve some of the black currants for decoration. Place the remainder in a bowl with the banana, orange peel and sugar and blend until the mixture has a smooth consistency.

Place the water into a saucepan and sprinkle the gelatine on top. Heat gently and stir until the gelatine is completely dissolved. The liquid must not boil. Allow to cool slightly then stir into the fruit mixture. Cover and refrigerate until it is much thicker.

Whisk the egg white until stiff, then gently fold it into the thickened fruit mixture with a metal spoon. Divide the mousse between four individual bowls. Swirl in the yoghurt to give a marbled effect, decorate with the remaining black currants and refrigerate until firm before serving.

Serves 4
Fat content per serving 1 g
Energy content per serving 195 kilocalories

10

PASTA, RICE AND OTHER CEREALS

PASTA

Although most people buy their pasta in packets from the supermarket, it has become increasingly easy to obtain freshly made pasta from delicatessens and specialist shops. Furthermore, many people have discovered how easy it is to make their own. Whichever source you use, pasta should be a staple ingredient of a low-fat diet: it is easy to cook; it has a very low fat content; it has a very high carbohydrate content; and if you buy wholemeal pasta it has a high fibre content.

Recipes for making your own pasta are not included here, as there are plenty of authentic recipes elsewhere. Suffice it to say that when you cook pasta you should use a large quantity of salted boiling water; if you use a small quantity of water you increase the chances of the pasta sticking together.

Dried pasta from the packet will need eight to 12 minutes boiling, depending on the type of pasta. Freshly made pasta will need considerably less time, perhaps only a minute. Whatever the variety, you should always test the pasta before draining; it should have a bit of bite, and should certainly not be soggy and sticky. Once it has been drained it should have the accompanying sauce stirred in or poured over it immediately; if not it should be gently tossed in a very small amount of oil to prevent the individual pieces sticking together.

You will find various recipes using pasta scattered throughout this book. What follows is a handful of basic sauce recipes; these sauces can be cooked easily and added to a bowl of pasta to provide a quick yet filling meal, accompanied by some vegetables or a salad.

Fat content per 3 oz (75 g) uncooked pasta serving 2 g
Energy content per 3 oz (75 g) uncooked pasta serving 245 kilocalories

TOMATO SAUCE
This is probably the simplest and cheapest pasta sauce to make, yet one of the tastiest.

> $1/2$ teaspoon olive oil
> 1 small onion, finely chopped
> 2 lb (1 kg) tomatoes or 2 × 14-oz (400-g) cans of
>   tomatoes
> 1 clove garlic, crushed
> 2 tablespoons freshly chopped parsley
> 1 tablespoon freshly chopped basil, if available
> 3 tablespoons red wine
> salt and freshly milled black pepper

Heat the oil in a heavy bottomed saucepan and cook the onion until it is soft and golden. Add the tomatoes, garlic, parsley, basil and red wine. Season with salt and pepper to taste, and cook over a high heat for about 10 minutes, stirring with a fork to break up the tomatoes.

Mash or sieve the sauce or purée in a blender. Return the sauce to the pan. Reduce the liquid content further if necessary by cooking the sauce over a high heat. Pour over a bowl of cooked pasta and serve immediately.

Serves 6
Fat content per serving 0.5 g
Energy content per serving 30 kilocalories

TOMATO AND VEGETABLE SAUCE

This is a variation on basic tomato sauce, using less tomatoes and some other vegetables.

$1/2$ teaspoon olive oil
1 large onion, chopped
2 carrots, scrubbed and chopped
1 stick celery, chopped
1 lb (450 g) tomatoes or 1 × 14-oz (400-g) can
    tomatoes
2 tablespoons tomato purée
4 oz (100 g) mushrooms, chopped
1 clove garlic, crushed
2 tablespoons freshly chopped parsley
1 tablespoon freshly chopped basil, if available
$1/4$ pint (150 ml) red wine
salt and freshly milled black pepper

Heat the oil in a heavy-bottomed saucepan and cook the onion gently until it softens. Add the carrots and celery and cook for a further five minutes. Add the tomatoes, tomato purée, mushrooms, garlic, parsley, basil and red wine. Bring to the boil, reduce the heat and simmer with the lid off for 20 minutes.

Mash the sauce in the pan or purée in a blender and return to the heat. Simmer for a further 10 minutes if necessary to reduce the liquid content – the consistency should be that of a thick purée. Season with salt and pepper to taste. Pour over cooked pasta and serve.

Serves 6
Fat content per serving 1 g
Energy content per serving 51 kilocalories

MUSHROOM SAUCE

$1/2$ teaspoon olive oil
1 onion, chopped
2 tablespoons freshly chopped parsley
1 clove garlic, crushed

1 tablespoon flour
1 lb (450 g) mushrooms, sliced
salt and freshly milled black pepper

Heat the oil in a frying pan and add the onion. Cook gently until it begins to soften, then add the parsley and garlic. Sprinkle over the flour and incorporate it into the ingredients in the pan. Add the mushrooms. Stirring gently with a spatula, simmer in the juice that comes from the mushrooms for five minutes, by which time the flour will have combined with the juices to form a thickened sauce. Remove the pan from the heat, season to taste and pour over freshly cooked pasta.

Serves 4
Fat content per serving 1.5 g
Energy content per serving 44 kilocalories

SEAFOOD SAUCE
While this recipe includes tuna and shrimps, other varieties of seafood such as mussels, clams or crabmeat can easily be added or substituted.

$^{1}/_{2}$ teaspoon olive oil
1 onion, chopped
2 carrots, scrubbed and chopped
2 sticks celery, chopped
1 clove garlic, crushed
$^{1}/_{4}$ pint (150 ml) medium dry white wine
6 oz (175 g) mushrooms, chopped
1 tablespoon freshly chopped herbs, e.g. parsley,
*   marjoram, thyme*
salt and freshly milled black pepper
1 × 6$^{1}/_{2}$-oz (185-g) can tuna in brine, drained
4 oz (100 g) peeled and cooked shrimps

Heat the oil in a large heavy-bottomed saucepan and cook the onion gently until it softens. Add the carrots, celery and garlic, cook for five minutes, then add the wine and the mushrooms. Cook fast with the lid off for 15–20 minutes until the carrot and celery are soft and the liquid has reduced considerably.

Remove the pan from the heat. Purée the sauce in a food mill, blender or processor. Return the purée to a clean saucepan and reduce further if necessary over a high heat. Add the herbs, salt and pepper to taste, and cook for a further two to three minutes. Fold in the tuna chunks and shrimps, stirring carefully so as not to break up the tuna too much. Heat through before pouring over freshly cooked pasta. Serve immediately.

Serves 4
Fat content per serving 7 g
Energy content per serving 142 kilocalories

BOLOGNESE SAUCE
This is a simple version of the classic Bolognese sauce, adapted from the ragú described in the next recipe, which is closer to the real thing.

½ teaspoon olive oil
1 onion, chopped
1 carrot, sliced finely
1 stick celery, chopped finely
8 oz (225 g) very lean minced beef
1 tablespoon wholemeal flour
1 tablespoon tomato purée
¾ pint (450 ml) meat or vegetable stock
salt and freshly ground black pepper

In a saucepan heat the olive oil and fry the onion gently until golden. Add the carrot and celery and cook for another five minutes. Add the mince to the pan, stirring and breaking up the meat with a fork until it has browned. Remove from the heat, allow to stand for 10–15 minutes, then lift off any fat from the surface with a sheet of kitchen paper.

Sprinkle the flour over the sauce. Stir in and replace the saucepan over a moderate heat. Add the tomato purée, stock and seasoning. Cover and simmer for 30 minutes until the sauce is rich and thick. It may be used immediately, or allowed to cool and reheated the next day. Sauces like this one freeze successfully.

Serves 4
Fat content per serving 5 g
Energy content per serving 108 kilocalories

RAGÚ
This is a real Bolognese sauce, but with a lower fat content than the traditional version.

> *¹/₂ teaspoon olive oil*
> *1 onion, chopped*
> *1 large carrot, finely sliced*
> *1 stick celery, finely chopped*
> *8 oz (225 g) very lean minced beef*
> *2 oz (50 g) chicken livers, chopped finely*
> *4 oz (100 g) very lean bacon or ham, all visible fat removed, chopped*
> *1 tablespoon tomato purée*
> *¹/₄ pint (150 ml) medium dry white wine*
> *¹/₂ pint (300 ml) meat or vegetable stock*
> *pinch of ground nutmeg*
> *salt and freshly milled black pepper*

In a large saucepan heat the olive oil and cook the onion gently until golden. Add the carrot and celery and cook for five minutes more. Add the minced beef, chicken livers and bacon or ham, stirring until they are nicely browned. Remove the pan from the heat and leave to stand for 10–15 minutes. Remove any fat from the surface with a sheet of kitchen paper.

Replace the pan over moderate heat. Stir in the tomato purée, wine, stock, nutmeg and seasoning. Bring to the boil, reduce the heat, cover and simmer for 30 minutes to an hour. Pour over freshly cooked pasta or use to make lasagne.

Serves 6
Fat content per serving 5 g
Energy content per serving 114 kilocalories

RICE

The three best known types of rice are long grain white rice, brown rice and pudding rice. There are, however, quite a few other varieties, including the mis-named wild rice, which is in fact a wild aquatic grass which takes twice as long to cook as rice.

Rice can be cooked in one of three ways:

- Wash the rice two or three times in cold water, then drain well. Place the rice in a saucepan with an equal volume of water, bring to the boil and let it boil uncovered for two minutes. Cover and simmer for 15 minutes. Do not remove the lid during this time. The rice is now ready for serving.

- Add the rice to a large volume of boiling water, bring the water back to the boil and boil with the lid off for 15 minutes. Drain and rinse through with boiling water. Serve.

- Add one part of rice to two parts of boiling water, bring back to the boil, cover and simmer for 30 minutes, by which time the rice will be cooked. This method is best for brown rice.

Fat content per 2½oz (65 g) uncooked serving 1.3 g
Energy content per 2½oz (65 g) uncooked serving 227 kilocalories

RISOTTO
Risotto is a slightly more elaborate way of cooking rice; it is a delicious accompaniment to many stews and casseroles. If you can, try it with Arborio rice, the kind traditionally used in italy.

1 teaspoon mono-unsaturated or polyunsaturated oil
1 onion, sliced

1 lb (450 g) long grain rice
¼ pint (150 ml) dry white wine
2¼ pints (1.25 litres) vegetable or chicken stock
salt and pepper to taste

Heat the oil in a heavy-bottomed saucepan and fry the
onion gently until it is soft. Stir in the rice, then add the
wine. Cook for two to three minutes, then add the stock
and seasoning and bring to the boil. Cover and simmer for
30 minutes. Test a few grains of rice. They should yield to
the bite without being mushy. Cook for a few more
minutes if necessary, then serve immediately.

Serves 6
Fat content per serving 4 g
Energy content per serving 300 kilocalories

RICE PILAF
This simple rice pilaf can be used as an accompaniment to
any number of meat and vegetarian dishes.

1 teaspoon mono-unsaturated or polyunsaturated oil
1 onion, chopped
10 oz (275 g) long grain rice
1 pint (600 ml) vegetable or chicken stock
4 oz (100 g) sultanas
4 oz (100 g) chopped walnuts
1 tablespoon freshly chopped parsley
1 teaspoon lemon juice
salt and pepper to taste

Heat the oil in a heavy-bottomed saucepan and fry the
onion gently until it is soft. Add the rice and cook for five
minutes, stirring frequently. Pour on the stock and bring
to the boil, stirring continuously. Cover and simmer for 30
minutes, leaving the lid in place; carefully test if the rice is
cooked and, if not, replace the lid for another few
minutes.

When the rice is cooked stir in the sultanas, walnuts,
parsley, lemon juice and seasoning. Heat through gently
and serve.

Serves 6
Fat content per serving 11 g
Energy content per serving 308 kilocalories

INDIAN BROWN RICE
The brown rice in this recipe refers to the colour of the cooked rice, not the raw rice grains. It is originally an accompaniment to *dhan sak*, the Parsee curry from Bombay, but is equally good with other curries or spicy dishes.

> 1 teaspoon mono-unsaturated or polyunsaturated oil
> 2 onions, finely chopped
> 12 cardamoms, cracked open with your thumbnail
> 4 × 1 in (4 × 2.5 cm) pieces of cinnamon, broken
> 12 cloves
> 7 black peppercorns
> salt to taste
> 1 teaspoon muscovado sugar
> 10 oz (275 g) long grain brown rice
> 1 pint (600 ml) water

Heat the oil in a flameproof casserole and fry the onion gently until it is golden. Put the cardamoms, pieces of cinnamon, cloves and peppercorns in a (clean) electric coffee mill and process for a few seconds. Add these ground spices to the onions with the salt and sugar. Cook until the onions start to darken in colour, but do not let them burn.

Add the water to the casserole, bring to the boil and simmer for two to three minutes. Tip in the rice and bring back to the boil. Cover the casserole and put in a preheated oven, gas mark 4 (180°C, 350°F), for 30 minutes. Remove from the oven and allow to stand for five to 10 minutes before serving.

Serves 4
Fat content per recipe 5 g
Energy content per recipe 285 kilocalories

COUSCOUS

Couscous is a type of semolina, originally from Morocco. In north Africa it is cooked by steaming it for an hour or so, usually over the stew with which it is to be served. In this country it is invariably sold pre-cooked, which means it can be prepared merely by adding twice its volume of boiling water, covering it and leaving it for 10 minutes. Unfortunately this method sometimes leaves it rather sticky and stodgy; steaming avoids this problem. If you do not have a steamer, you will need a colander or sieve that fits over a saucepan of boiling water.

STEAMED COUSCOUS

> *12 oz (350 g) couscous*
> *1/2 teaspoon olive oil*
> *salt to taste*

Bring the water in the steamer or saucepan to the boil. If the holes in the top part of the steamer, colander or sieve are too big (couscous is a fine cereal), arrange a piece of immaculately clean muslin inside.

   Put the couscous into the steamer, colander or sieve, and set it over the boiling water. Cover and steam for 10 minutes. Use a fork to fluff up the grains, then steam for another 10 minutes, by which time the grains should be tender and soft; if not, fluff up again and cook further.

   Stir in the olive oil and salt, and turn out on to a heated serving dish.

Serves 4
Fat content per serving 2 g
Energy content per serving 206 kilocalories

TABBOULEH

This is a classic salad from the Arab world. It can be made with cracked (Bulgar) wheat, but this version with couscous is much quicker to prepare. Ideally it should be made with coriander leaf, but if you cannot obtain coriander then flat-leaved parsley is almost as good.

> *4 oz (100 g) couscous*
> *2 teaspoons olive oil*
> *juice of 1 lemon*
> *8 oz (225 g) tomatoes, coarsely chopped*
> *5 oz (150 g) cucumber, coarsely chopped*
> *salt and freshly milled black pepper*
> *2 tablespoons freshly chopped mint*
> *2 teaspoons freshly chopped coriander leaf or 1 table-*
> *   spoon freshly chopped flat-leaf parsley*

Pour the couscous into a salad bowl, add the olive oil and lemon juice and stir well. Add the tomato and cucumber and stir again thoroughly. Cover and leave for 30 minutes; stir again. After a further 30 minutes the couscous should have absorbed the oil, lemon juice, and juice from the tomatoes and cucumber in such a way that each grain is soft yet separate.

Add salt and pepper to taste. Stir in the chopped mint and coriander or parsley leaves. Stand for 10 minutes before serving, perhaps with a green salad.

Serves 4
Fat content per serving 3 g
Energy content per serving 94 kilocalories

MILLET

Millet is if anything even less well known than couscous, although it is very nutritious and has a delicious nutty taste. It is available in most health food stores.

SAVOURY MILLET

> *1 teaspoon mono-unsaturated or polyunsaturated oil*
> *1 onion, sliced*
> *1 stick celery, chopped*

1 green pepper, cored, deseeded and chopped
10 oz (275 g) millet
1 teaspoon poppy seeds
24 fl oz (720 ml) water
salt and pepper to taste

Heat the oil in a flameproof casserole and fry the onion gently until it is golden. Add the celery and green pepper and continue cooking for two to three minutes. Add the millet and poppy seeds, and increase the heat. Continue to cook, stirring continuously, until the millet has turned golden and smells nutty.

Add the water, salt and pepper and bring to the boil. Cover the casserole and transfer to a preheated oven, gas mark 4 (180°C, 350°F), for 30 minutes. Remove from the oven, and serve hot if you wish or let the millet cool, fork it through to separate the grains, then warm through again gently before serving.

Serves 4
Fat content per serving 3 g
Energy content per serving 250 kilocalories

MILLET AND SULTANA PUDDING
Millet need not only be used as an accompaniment for savoury dishes; it can also be used in delicious puddings.

1/2 teaspoon mono-unsaturated or polyunsaturated oil
2 oz (50 g) chopped almonds
6 oz (175 g) millet
1 1/2 pints (900 ml) skimmed milk
2 oz (50 g) demerara sugar
2 oz (50 g) sultanas
1 teaspoon ground cinnamon

Heat the oil in a saucepan and fry the almonds and millet gently together until they are golden. Add the milk, sugar and sultanas and bring to the boil. Reduce the heat and simmer for five minutes. Pour into an ovenproof dish,

145

sprinkle over the cinnamon and bake in a preheated oven, gas mark 3 (160°C, 325°F), for one hour.

Serves 4
Fat content per serving 9 g
Energy content per serving 355 kilocalories

OTHER WHOLE GRAINS

There are many other whole and cracked grains that you can buy, some more readily available than others – Bulgar (or cracked) wheat, buckwheat, barley, rye, whole wheat, to name but a few. All can be cooked by boiling in water, after which they can be added to various dishes, both hot and cold. Here are a couple of useful, delicious recipes; once you have got used to cooking with whole grains you will be able to find many more, and perhaps concoct some of your own.

BARLEY, VEGETABLE AND YOGHURT BAKE

8 oz (225 g) barley
1½ pints (900 ml) water
1 teaspoon mono-unsaturated or polyunsaturated oil
2 onions, chopped
8 oz (225 g) carrots, chopped
4 sticks celery, chopped
1 tablespoon soy sauce
2 tablespoons tomato purée
salt and pepper
8 oz (225 g) mushrooms, chopped coarsely
4 oz (100 g) virtually fat-free yoghurt
1 tablespoon self-raising flour
1 egg

In a heavy-bottomed saucepan set over a moderate heat, toast the barley until it smells nutty – about three to five minutes. Add the water, bring to the boil and simmer for 45 minutes. Set to one side.

146

In a flameproof casserole heat the oil and fry the onion gently until it is golden. Add the carrots and celery and continue cooking for five minutes. Add the barley, soy sauce, tomato purée and salt and pepper to taste. Stir well and let the mixture heat through. Lastly stir in the mushrooms, and with a spatula smooth over the surface of the contents of the casserole.

In a bowl combine the yoghurt and flour. Beat in the egg. Pour this mixture over the surface of the casserole, cover and bake in a preheated oven, gas mark 5 (190°C, 375°F), for 30 minutes or until the yoghurt topping has set. Serve hot.

Serves 4
Fat content per serving 5 g
Energy content per serving 305 kilocalories

CRACKED WHEAT AND WALNUTS

This can be served as a winter salad, or warmed through to make an accompaniment to hot dishes.

> *8 oz (225 g) cracked (Bulgar) wheat*
> *1 pint (600 ml) boiling water*
> *½ teaspoon olive oil*
> *1 onion, sliced*
> *4 oz (100 g) tomato purée*
> *½ teaspoon ground cinnamon*
> *1 teaspoon ground cumin*
> *2 teaspoons coriander seeds*
> *1 tablespoon freshly chopped mint or parsley*
> *juice of 1 lemon*
> *4 oz (100 g) walnuts, chopped*

Put the cracked wheat in a bowl, pour over the boiling water, stir, cover and leave for 30 minutes. By this time the cracked wheat should have absorbed all the water. If not, drain and squeeze out the surplus water.

Heat the oil in a frying pan and fry the onion gently until soft and golden. Combine the cracked wheat with the onion and all the remaining ingredients in a serving bowl.

Leave to stand for at least one hour for the flavours to amalgamate, stirring occasionally.

Serves 4
Fat content per serving 16 g
Energy content per serving 364 kilocalories

11

VEGETABLES AND SALADS

POTATOES

People on slimming diets were once counselled to steer clear of potatoes; they were regarded as heavy, stodgy vegetables that were bound to put the weight on. Now the advice is almost the opposite – cut down on the energy-rich fatty foods that are likely to increase your weight and raise your blood cholesterol level, and instead eat more potatoes and other vegetables that have no fat and are short on calories.

The one problem with potatoes is that they are often cooked or served with fats or oils – roast potatoes, chips, mashed potatoes with butter and milk, jacket potatoes with butter and cheese. But it doesn't have to be like this, and in the following pages we give you some low-fat ideas for cooking and serving potatoes.

Boiled potatoes

Boil potatoes in their skins, whenever possible, as this gives them a lot more flavour and increases the fibre content. And always try to serve boiled potatoes with dishes or other vegetables that have a sauce; this will ensure that there is some fluid to accompany the potatoes, and do away with the need for butter to be added to them.

If you add chopped mint to boiled potatoes, make sure you add it just as you serve them; then it remains green and fresh. If you add it five or 10 minutes before serving the potatoes the mint leaves go dark and lose a lot of their flavour.

Mashed potato

Instead of mashing potatoes with milk and margarine or butter, try using a couple of spoons of plain virtually fat-free yoghurt or fromage frais.

To make really fine mashed potatoes, do not cook them so long that they fall apart, and make certain that they are as dry as possible once you've drained them. Mash them on their own, then slowly add hot skimmed milk, whisking them with a fork all the while. Once you have beaten in enough milk, and the yoghurt or fromage frais if you want, continue whisking for another two to three minutes; the final product should be more of a light purée than a heavy stodge.

Jacket potatoes

Jacket potatoes require little preparation other than a good scrubbing before they are popped into the oven, although pushing a metal skewer through the centre of each one will speed up the cooking process by conducting heat into the centre more rapidly.

For serving jacket potatoes, again try to use dishes with a sauce; perhaps make extra sauce, so that a jug of it is available to pour over the potatoes. Alternatively you can use plain virtually fat-free yoghurt or fromage frais again, or concoct your own fillings along the lines of those given for sandwich fillings (Chapter 7).

Roast potatoes

You can dry-roast potatoes by bringing them to the boil, draining well, sprinkling with a little salt, arranging on a non-stick baking tray and cooking at gas mark 6 (220°C, 400°F), for at least one hour.

Alternatively, bring them to the boil, drain very well,

arrange on a non-stick baking tray and brush with a little mono-unsaturated or polyunsaturated oil before cooking. A little oil goes a long way used like this, and still gives you the crisp exterior associated with roast potatoes. If you like, you can sprinkle herbs over the potatoes before they go into the oven.

BAKED POTATOES AND ONION
King Edward potatoes are the best variety for this dish.

> 1 lb (450 g) peeled potatoes, sliced as thinly as possible
> 1 clove garlic
> 2 onions, sliced as thinly as possible
> salt and freshly milled black pepper
> 1/2 pint (300 ml) skimmed milk
> 4 oz (100 g) plain virtually fat-free yoghurt or fromage frais

Rinse the sliced potatoes under cold water and dry thoroughly on kitchen paper or a tea towel.

Lightly grease a shallow ovenproof dish and rub the inside of the dish with the garlic clove cut in two. Arrange the potato and onion slices in layers, seasoning each layer.

In a mixing bowl beat together the milk and the yoghurt or fromage frais. Pour this mixture over the potatoes and onions – they should be completely covered, and the dish should be full to within a 1/2 inch (1 cm) of the top. Cook, uncovered, in a preheated oven, gas mark 2 (150°C, 300°F), for 1 1/2 hours, then turn the oven up high for 10 minutes or so to form a crust on the top. Serve straight from the dish.

Serves 4
Fat content per serving 0.5 g
Energy content per serving 155 kilocalories

VEGETABLES

RATATOUILLE

There are probably as many variations of this classic French dish as there are households in the south of France, but all use roughly the same mix of vegetables. The classic version uses a lot of olive oil; obviously, this has been cut down in the version below.

> 2 large aubergines, sliced then cubed
> 2 medium courgettes, sliced then cubed
> 2 teaspoons olive oil
> 4 medium onions, sliced
> 2 large red peppers, cored, deseeded and sliced
> 2 cloves garlic, crushed
> 1/4 pint (150 ml) red wine
> 4 large tomatoes, sliced or 1 × 14-oz (400-g) can tomatoes
> 1 teaspoon coriander seeds, crushed in a pestle and mortar
> freshly milled black pepper
> salt
> 2 teaspoons freshly chopped basil leaves or 1 tablespoon freshly chopped parsley

Place the chopped aubergines and courgettes in a colander, sprinkle with salt and place a weighted plate on top. Leave for one to two hours, rinse under cold running water and drain well. This will remove the excess liquid from these vegetables.

Heat the olive oil in a large heavy-bottomed saucepan or a cast-iron casserole. Fry the onions gently until they are soft. Add the aubergines, courgettes, peppers, garlic and wine, cover and cook for about 30 minutes. Add the tomatoes, crushed coriander seeds, salt and pepper to taste, and cook uncovered for a further 30 minutes, until the liquid has reduced – the vegetables should be soft but should not fall apart. Finally stir in the basil or parsley.

Serve as a starter, as an accompaniment to hot dishes,

as a sauce, e.g. for pasta, or cold as an accompaniment to cold dishes.

Serves 6
Fat content per serving 2 g
Energy content per serving 87 kilocalories

CARROTS IN HONEY

This is a particularly useful recipe towards the end of the winter, when what carrots that are available tend to have little flavour.

> *1 lb (450 g) carrots, scrubbed and sliced*
> *¹/₂ teaspoon olive oil*
> *1 teaspoon honey*
> *freshly milled black pepper*
> *¹/₂ teaspoon cumin seeds*

Put the carrots in a saucepan, barely cover with water, add the olive oil and the honey, cover and bring to the boil. Remove the saucepan lid and continue boiling so that the liquid gradually reduces as the carrots cook – they should be cooked by the time the liquid has reduced to a syrup.

Once the carrots are cooked add pepper to taste, sprinkle over the cumin seeds and cook for a further one to two minutes. Serve hot.

One teaspoon of freshly chopped parsley, if available, may be substituted for the cumin seeds.

Serves 4
Fat content per serving 1 g
Energy content per serving 37 kilocalories

SPICY CABBAGE

This recipe works equally well with red or white cabbage, but it is best to use one of the solid compact varieties – varieties with loose leaves cook down too much. If you find the taste of the juniper berries too astringent, these may be omitted.

1 small or ½ a large cabbage
1 onion, sliced
1 large or 2 small cooking apples, cored and sliced
1 teaspoon rosemary, chopped
1 teaspoon juniper berries (optional)
   pepper
1 tablespoon clear honey
1 tablespoon white or red wine vinegar
1 tablespoon sweet wine

Before slicing the cabbage remove the stalk. Cut the
cabbage in quarters and cut out the tough core of each
piece. Slice the cabbage evenly.

Arrange the cabbage, onion and apple in layers in an
ovenproof casserole. Sprinkle over the chopped rosemary,
juniper berries and pepper to taste. Pour over the honey,
vinegar and wine. Cover and cook in a preheated oven,
gas mark 2 (150°C, 300°F), for two to three hours. Serve
hot.

Serves 4
Fat content per serving – none
Energy content per serving 93 kilocalories

JERUSALEM ARTICHOKES IN TOMATO SAUCE
Jerusalem artichokes are not widely available – despite the
fact that they are idiot-proof to grow – and are a bit fiddly
to peel. They are a very good winter vegetable, though,
with a sweet and nutty taste. Drop the peeled artichokes in
water to which a little lemon juice has been added, to
prevent discoloration.

1½lb (750g) Jerusalem artichokes, peeled and
   halved
½ teaspoon mono-unsaturated or polyunsaturated oil
3 large tomatoes, chopped
2 teaspoons tomato purée
1 teaspoon freshly chopped basil or marjoram
1 clove garlic, crushed
freshly milled black pepper

154

Put the artichokes in a saucepan, barely cover with water and bring to the boil. Reduce the heat and simmer until they are just done – 15–20 minutes should be enough. If they start floating and breaking up you have cooked them for too long. Drain and set to one side.

Place the oil in a clean saucepan set over moderate heat. Add the tomatoes. When the tomatoes are bubbling add the artichokes, tomato purée, basil or marjoram, the garlic and pepper to taste. Combine the ingredients thoroughly, then simmer over a low heat until the tomato sauce has reduced to thick purée and the artichokes are tender.

Serves 6
Fat content per serving 1 g
Energy content per serving 39 kilocalories

CAULIFLOWER AND POTATO IN YOGHURT

Mashed potatoes are a common accompaniment to winter dishes, but mashed cauliflower will come as a surprise.

> *1 medium cauliflower, leaves removed*
> *1½lb (750g) potatoes, peeled*
> *4oz (100g) virtually fat-free yoghurt*
> *pinch of ground nutmeg*
> *salt and freshly ground black pepper*
> *2oz (50g) porridge oats*
> *1 teaspoon sesame seeds*

Break or cut the cauliflower up into florets of equal size and boil or steam them until soft – about 10 minutes. Drain and set to one side.

Boil the potatoes until they are cooked, drain and tip into a bowl. Add the cauliflower and mash thoroughly. Add the yoghurt and nutmeg, salt and pepper to taste, and beat thoroughly with a fork.

Spoon the mixture into an ovenproof dish. Sprinkle the porridge oats and sesame seeds on top and bake in a preheated oven, gas mark 4 (180°C, 350°F), for 30 minutes or until the oats are golden.

Serves 6
Fat content per serving 1.5 g
Energy content per serving 176 kilocalories

GRATED PARSNIP AND CARROT
This is an excellent way of using carrots and parsnips when they are coming to the end of their season, or you can equally well substitute swede or turnip for the parsnip.

>   *1 teaspoon mono-unsaturated or polyunsaturated oil*
>   *2 teaspoons dark brown sugar*
>   *1 lb (450 g) carrots, scrubbed and grated*
>   *1 lb (450 g) parsnips, scrubbed, peeled if necessary, and grated*
>   *¹/₂ teaspoon ground nutmeg*
>   *salt and freshly milled black pepper*

Heat the oil in a large heavy-bottomed saucepan. Add the sugar, grated carrot and parsnip, and the nutmeg. Stir well and cook over a low heat for 15–20 minutes, or until the carrots and parsnips are soft. Season to taste and serve hot.

Serves 6
Fat content per serving 1 g
Energy content per serving 103 kilocalories

AUBERGINES IN TOMATO SAUCE

>   *1 teaspoon olive oil*
>   *1 medium onion, chopped*
>   *1 lb (450 g) tomatoes, chopped or 1 × 14-oz (400 g) can tomatoes, drained and chopped*
>   *1 tablespoon freshly chopped parsley*
>   *1 teaspoon freshly chopped basil*
>   *salt and freshly milled black pepper*
>   *2 aubergines, sliced thickly*

Heat the oil in a saucepan and cook the onion gently until soft. Add the tomatoes and herbs and simmer until the tomatoes are falling apart and much of the liquid has reduced. Remove the pan from the heat. Purée the sauce in a food mill, blender or food processor. Season to taste.

Blanch the aubergine slices in boiling salted water for two to three minutes. Drain and pat dry with kitchen paper. Arrange the aubergine slices in a single layer in a large shallow baking dish or tray. Pour over the tomato sauce, making sure all the slices are covered. Bake in a preheated oven, gas mark 2 (150°C, 300°F), for one hour. Serve hot or warm.

Serves 4
Fat content per serving 1.5 g
Energy content per serving 65 kilocalories

SALADS

Salads are often referred to as 'health foods' or 'rabbit food' – insubstantial, and the main constituent of unfortunate slimmers' diets. The fact is that salads can be very substantial, to the extent that they can be used as the main part of a meal rather than as an accompaniment. Alternatively, because they are so attractive, they can be used as starters or as a separate course after the main meal.

The secret of good salads is to choose very fresh unblemished ingredients, and to handle them as little as possible during preparation. Some salads should be allowed time to relax once prepared, so that the flavours blend together well: others are better served straight away, retaining maximum crispness and freshness. Forget about so-called salads made up of a dull mixture of anything left over in the refrigerator, maybe some cold vegetables, plus a can of something, the sad collection disguised with salad cream or mayonnaise. The following recipes are fresh, healthy and interesting; in particular, none of them involves salad cream or mayonnaise, both of which have a very high fat content and a very high saturated fat content.

These salads provide maximum nutrition in exciting ways. And once you realise that there is far more to a salad than a limp lettuce, or an over-ripe tomato and a soft cucumber you'll discover all sorts of combinations of vegetables, fruits, spices and fresh herbs, dressed with different types of oils and vinegars, producing wholesome filling dishes that all the family will enjoy.

Just one point to remember. Do try and use up a salad at the latest the day after it is made, as the enjoyment is derived from a salad's freshness; the only exceptions to this rule are salads based on potato, pasta, rice or other grains.

BROWN RICE AND PEANUT SALAD

Salad
    6 oz (175 g) cooked long grain brown rice
    4 oz (100 g) unsalted peanuts
    1 large carrot, scrubbed and grated
    1 bunch spring onions, cleaned and chopped
    1 tablespoon freshly chopped parsley
Dressing
    3 tablespoons olive oil
    3 tablespoons lemon juice
    1 tablespoon white wine vinegar
    5 oz (150 g) plain virtually fat-free yoghurt
    1 tablespoon apple juice
    1 clove garlic, crushed
    salt and freshly milled black pepper

Combine all the salad ingredients in a large bowl. Put all the ingredients for the dressing in a screw-top jar and shake well for 30 seconds. Before serving, toss the salad with three to four tablespoons of the dressing.

Serves 4
Fat content per serving 25 g
Energy content per serving 347 kilocalories

FRUIT PASTA SALAD

8 oz (225 g) wholemeal pasta shells, twists or bows,
  cooked and drained
10 fl oz (300 ml) plain virtually fat-free yoghurt
2 tablespoons tomato purée
4 sticks celery, chopped
1 small can crushed pineapple in natural juice,
  drained and juice reserved
4 oz (100 g) dried apricots, chopped and soaked
  overnight in the pineapple juice
2 oz (50 g) dates, destoned and chopped
2 oz (50 g) raisins or sultanas
1 oz (25 g) toasted almonds
freshly milled black pepper

In a large bowl stir together the pasta, yoghurt, tomato
purée, celery and all the fruits. Sprinkle the almonds on
top and grind the pepper over the salad before serving.

Serves 6
Fat content per serving 3 g
Energy content per serving 207 kilocalories

BEANY SALAD

1 × 14-oz (400-g) can red kidney beans, drained and
  rinsed
1 × 14-oz (400-g) can chickpeas, drained and rinsed
8 oz (225 g) broad beans, cooked and cooled
8 oz (225 g) runner or French beans, cooked and
  cooled
5 oz (150 g) plain virtually fat-free yoghurt
juice of 1/2 a lemon
1 tablespoon wholegrain mustard
1 tablespoon freshly chopped parsley
freshly milled black pepper

Combine all the beans and chickpeas in a bowl. In a
separate bowl mix the yoghurt with the lemon juice and

mustard. Pour this dressing over the beans and mix well.
Sprinkle with parsley and black pepper and serve.

Serves 6
Fat content per serving 4 g
Energy content per serving 198 kilocalories

SWEETCORN AND PEPPER SALAD

> *5 oz (150 g) cooked frozen sweetcorn kernels*
> *1 onion, chopped very finely*
> *1 small red pepper, cored, deseeded and chopped*
> *1 small green pepper, cored, deseeded and chopped*
> *1 small yellow pepper, cored, deseeded and chopped*
> *2 oz (50 g) sultanas*
> *2 oz (50 g) walnuts, chopped*
> *freshly milled black pepper*

Combine all the ingredients in a large bowl and grind the
pepper over them before serving.

Serves 4
Fat content per serving 7 g
Energy content per serving 146 kilocalories

FENNEL AND FRUIT SALAD

> Salad
> > *2 medium fennel bulbs, peeled and chopped*
> > *1 cos lettuce, shredded*
> > *2 kiwi fruit, peeled and thinly sliced*
> > *2 oranges, peeled, pith removed, sliced*
> > *1 bunch watercress, washed and drained*
> > *2 oz (50 g) walnut halves*
> Dressing
> > *4 oz (100 g) fresh or frozen raspberries, blended until
> > smooth*
> > *3 tablespoons walnut oil*

Toss the fennel and lettuce together in a large bowl. Place

the orange and kiwi slices overlapping around the edge of a large, shallow serving dish. Arrange the watercress just inside the ring of fruit. Fill the centre with the fennel and lettuce and scatter the nuts over the top. Dribble over two to three tablespoons of the dressing and chill well before serving.

Serves 4
Fat content per serving 15 g
Energy content per serving 250 kilocalories

CELERIAC, CARROT AND SESAME SALAD

1 small celeriac, peeled and grated
8 oz (225 g) carrots, scrubbed and grated
1 onion, chopped
3 oz (75 g) raisins
1 tablespoon sesame seeds, toasted
juice of 1 lemon
5 oz (150 g) plain virtually fat-free yoghurt

Combine all the ingredients in a large bowl and serve immediately.

Serves 4
Fat content per serving 2.5 g
Energy content per serving 128 kilocalories

BEETROOT AND GRAPEFRUIT SALAD

8 oz (225 g) cooked beetroot, skinned and diced
1 large grapefruit, peeled, pith removed and segments
*   skinned*
1 orange, peeled, pith removed and segments skinned
1 small onion, chopped
3 sticks celery, chopped
2 oz (50 g) hazelnuts, chopped
juice of 1 lemon
1 tablespoon freshly chopped chives
freshly milled black pepper

161

In a large bowl combine all the ingredients except the chives and pepper. Sprinkle the chives on top, grind over pepper to taste and serve.

Serves 4
Fat content per serving 4.5 g
Energy content per serving 110 kilocalories

SPINACH, CHEESE AND ALMOND SALAD

> 8 oz (225 g) young spinach leaves, washed and shredded
> small head of radicchio, washed and shredded
> 8 oz (225 g) very-low-fat cottage cheese
> 5 oz (150 g) cooked frozen sweetcorn kernels
> 1 clove garlic, crushed
> 2 oz (50 g) toasted almonds
> freshly ground black pepper

Place the spinach and radicchio in a large bowl. Combine the cottage cheese with the sweetcorn kernels and garlic. Spoon this mixture over the salad leaves and toss gently to coat them evenly. Strew the toasted almonds on top, add a few grinds of pepper and serve.

Serves 6
Fat content per serving 6.5 g
Energy content per serving 121 kilocalories

ORIENTAL SALAD

Salad
> head of Chinese leaves, washed and shredded
> 4 oz (100 g) cooked frozen sweetcorn
> 2 oz (50 g) sprouted aduki beans
> 2 oz (50 g) sprouted alfalfa seeds
> 2 oz (50 g) bean sprouts
> 1 carton mustard and cress
> 2 tomatoes, sliced
> 1 tablespoon sesame seeds, toasted

162

Dressing

3 oz (75 g) plain virtually fat-free yoghurt
2 tablespoons tahini (sesame seed paste)
juice of 1/2 lemon
2 teaspoons soy sauce
1 teaspoon soft brown sugar
1/2 teaspoon ground ginger
freshly milled black pepper

Put the dressing ingredients in a screw-top jar and shake well, or combine them in a blender or food processor. Combine all the salad ingredients in a large bowl, pour over two to three tablespoons of the dressing and chill for at least two hours before serving.

Serves 6
Fat content per serving 4.5 g
Energy content per serving 134 kilocalories

RED SALAD

1 small head radicchio, washed and shredded
1 red pepper, cored, deseeded and chopped
4 tomatoes, quartered
6 oz (175 g) radishes, sliced
4 oz (100 g) spring onions, cleaned and chopped
2 oz (50 g) walnuts, chopped
2 tablespoons tarragon vinegar
freshly milled black pepper

Combine all the ingredients in a large bowl. Chill for two hours before serving.

Serves 4
Fat content per serving 7 g
Energy content per serving 120 kilocalories

BULGAR WHEAT SALAD

6 oz (175 g) Bulgar (cracked or nibbed) wheat
1 red pepper, cored, deseeded and chopped
1 green pepper, cored, deseeded and chopped
1 yellow pepper, cored, deseeded and chopped
1 onion, chopped
4 tablespoons coarsely chopped parsley
1 clove garlic, crushed
juice of 1 lemon
2 tablespoons olive or peanut (groundnut) oil
salt and freshly ground black pepper
2 tablespoons stoned black olives, to garnish

Wash the Bulgar wheat under cold running water in a large sieve. Still in the sieve, soak the wheat in a bowl of boiling water for 15–20 minutes or until the grains are soft. Lift the sieve out of the bowl and allow the wheat to drain well, squeezing out the last of the water.

Combine the peppers, onion, parsley, garlic, lemon juice, oil and seasoning in a large bowl. Stir in the wheat. Leave to stand for 30 minutes. Garnish with the olives to serve.

Serves 6
Fat content per serving 6.5 g
Energy content per serving 169 kilocalories

GREEK CHEESE SALAD

1 small head radicchio
1 lb (450 g) tomatoes, very roughly chopped
1/2 cucumber, very roughly chopped
1 red pepper, cored, deseeded and roughly chopped
1 green pepper, cored, deseeded and roughly chopped
8 oz (225 g) stoned black olives
1/2 lemon, thinly sliced
2 oz (50 g) feta cheese, crumbled
freshly ground black pepper
1 tablespoon olive oil

Separate out all the radicchio leaves, wash them well, pat dry and use to line a serving bowl. In a separate bowl combine all the ingredients except the olive oil, and arrange them on the bed of radicchio leaves. Spoon over the olive oil and serve.

Serves 6
Fat content per serving 9 g
Energy content per serving 116 kilocalories

GREEN SALAD

1 cos, iceberg, Webbs or other green lettuce, washed and shredded
8 oz (225 g) courgettes, washed and sliced thinly
2 green peppers, cored, deseeded and sliced
3 oz (75 g) spring or salad onions, trimmed and roughly chopped
4 oz (100 g) broad beans, cooked and cooled
2 green dessert apples, cored and sliced
2 oz (50 g) muscadet raisins
juice of 1 lemon

In a large salad bowl carefully combine all the ingredients. Serve immediately.

Serves 6
Fat content per serving 0.8 g
Energy content per serving 83 kilocalories

GARDEN SALAD

Salad
1 small lettuce, washed and shredded
1 carton mustard and cress
1/2 cucumber, diced
8 oz (225 g) tomatoes, sliced
3 oz (75 g) carrots, scrubbed and sliced
1 small onion, thinly sliced
2 oz (50 g) radishes, chopped

Dressing
> 5 tablespoons peanut (groundnut) oil
> 2 tablespoons lemon juice
> $^1/_2$ teaspoon mustard powder
> salt and freshly ground black pepper

Line a large bowl with the lettuce leaves. In a separate bowl combine the remaining salad ingredients. Arrange this mixture over the lettuce.

Put all the dressing ingredients into a screw-top jar and shake well, or combine in a blender or food processor. Pour two or three tablespoons of the dressing over the salad and serve.

Serves 6
Fat content per serving 13 g
Energy content per serving 145 kilocalories

POTATO SALAD

> 1 lb (450 g) new waxy potatoes, halved, boiled, drained and cooled
> 4 oz (100 g) plain virtually fat-free yoghurt
> 1 tablespoon olive oil
> 3 tablespoons freshly chopped chives
> salt and freshly milled black pepper

Dry the potatoes and place them in a serving bowl. Put the remaining ingredients in another bowl and beat together with a fork. Pour this dressing over the potatoes and mix carefully.

Serves 4
Fat content per serving 4 g
Energy content per serving 137 kilocalories

There are many variations on this basic potato salad. For a start, you could use very small potatoes and leave them whole, or larger potatoes and dice them. Add one or a number of the following:

- Chopped cucumber.
- Sliced gherkins.
- Cubed low-fat cheeses.
- Diced green, red and/or yellow pepper.
- Chopped celery.
- Chopped radishes.
- Thin slices of peeled orange, pith and skin removed.
- Halved pipped grapes.
- Raisins.
- Finely chopped onion, spring onion or shallot instead of the chives.

COLESLAW

4oz (100g) carrot, scrubbed and grated
4oz (100g) white cabbage, shredded
2oz (50g) celery, thinly sliced
4oz (100g) red apple, cored and thinly sliced
2oz (50g) green apple, cored and thinly sliced
3oz (75g) plain virtually fat-free yoghurt
2 tablespoons lemon juice
salt and freshly milled black pepper

Thoroughly combine all the ingredients in a bowl. Chill well in the refrigerator for two to four hours before serving.

Serves 4
Fat content per serving – trace
Energy content per serving 47 kilocalories

GREEN LENTIL SALAD

8oz (225g) green lentils, cooked and drained
2 large onions, chopped
2 cloves garlic, chopped
1 bunch fresh coriander leaf or watercress, chopped
juice of 1 lemon
3 tablespoons olive or peanut (groundnut) oil
salt and freshly milled black pepper

Combine all the ingredients in a bowl, cover and chill overnight before serving.

Serves 6
Fat content per serving 8 g
Energy content per serving 130 kilocalories

CHICKPEA, TOMATO AND MUSHROOM SALAD

1 × 14-oz (400-g) can chickpeas, drained and rinsed
1 lb (450 g) tomatoes, chopped
2 onions, chopped
4 oz (100 g) mushrooms, sliced
1 clove garlic, crushed
juice of ½ a lemon
1 teaspoon Dijon mustard
3 tablespoons walnut oil
1 tablespoon freshly chopped parsley, to garnish

In a large bowl, thoroughly mix all the ingredients except the parsley. Chill for two to four hours before serving with the parsley sprinkled on top.

Serves 6
Fat content per serving 10 g
Energy content per serving 195 kilocalories

CURRIED RICE SALAD

4 oz (100 g) brown rice, cooked and allowed to cool
4 oz (100 g) frozen mixed vegetables, cooked and allowed to cool
1 green pepper, cored, deseeded and chopped
1 red pepper, cored, deseeded and chopped
1 × 7-oz (200-g) can red kidney beans, drained and rinsed
2 oz (50 g) sultanas
4 oz (100 g) plain virtually fat-free fromage frais
1 teaspoon curry powder

In a large bowl combine all the ingredients except the fromage frais and the curry powder. In a separate bowl combine the fromage frais and the curry powder, mixing until smooth. Pour this mixture over the salad and blend thoroughly. Cover and chill for two to four hours before serving.

Serves 6
Fat content per serving 0.8 g
Energy content per serving 98 kilocalories

FENNEL AND TOMATO SALAD

> *2 fennel bulbs, sliced*
> *8 oz (225 g) tomatoes, sliced*
> *2 onions, sliced*
> *1 lettuce, washed and shredded*
> *2 tablespoons sunflower seeds*
> *1 tablespoon sesame seed oil*
> *salt and freshly milled black pepper*

Combine all the ingredients in a large bowl and serve immediately.

Serves 6
Fat content per serving 5 g
Energy content per serving 97 kilocalories

RED CABBAGE SALAD

> *2 oz (50 g) raisins*
> *8 tablespoons white wine vinegar*
> *12 oz (350 g) red cabbage, sliced*
> *2 green apples, cored and sliced*
> *1 onion, chopped*
> *salt and freshly milled black pepper*

In a bowl soak the raisins in the vinegar overnight. Drain if necessary, reserving the vinegar. Mix the cabbage, apples and onion in a serving bowl. Add the raisins, one tablespoon of the reserved vinegar (or to taste) and season to taste. Stir and serve.

Serves 6
Fat content per serving – none
Energy content per serving 75 kilocalories

BRIE AND BANANA SALAD

2 large firm bananas, sliced thickly
juice of 1 lemon
4 oz (100 g) Brie, cubed
1/2 cucumber, diced
4 tomatoes, roughly chopped
4 oz (100 g) grapes, halved and pipped
4 oz (100 g) plain virtually fat-free yoghurt
salt and freshly milled black pepper
1 tablespoon sesame seeds, toasted

Place the banana slices in a bowl with the lemon juice and stir gently. Place the chunks of Brie in the serving bowl with the banana and lemon juice. Add the cucumber, tomatoes, grapes and yoghurt and stir gently. Season to taste, sprinkle the sesame seeds over the salad and serve.

Serves 6
Fat content per serving 6 g
Energy content per serving 133 kilocalories

12

CAKES AND BAKING

PASTRY AND CRUMBLES

You will notice that even with the modifications we have introduced, pastry and crumble toppings are still relatively high in fat, so should not be regular features on your menus. For this reason few recipes are given here. One basic piece of advice is to use wholemeal flour wherever possible in your pastry.

SHORTCRUST PASTRY

Here we have used wholemeal flour, but a proportion of oat bran could be introduced (6oz/175g flour and 2oz/50g oat bran) to increase the soluble fibre content. More importantly, we have used rapeseed oil (the cheapest and least flavoured of the mono-unsaturated oils) instead of margarine or fat as this reduces the saturated fat content and increases the mono-unsaturate content significantly.

> *8oz (225g) wholemeal flour, sifted*
> *6 tablespoons rapeseed oil*
> *pinch of salt if necessary*
> *water to mix*

Place the flour in a mixing bowl, make a well in the centre

and pour in the oil. Add the salt, then fork the oil into the flour until it resembles breadcrumbs. Sprinkle on just enough water to make a soft dough, and mix with a fork. Cover and place in the refrigerator for 15–20 minutes. Roll out on a floured surface and bake blind in a preheated oven, gas mark 6 (200°C, 400°F), for 15 minutes.

Makes a pastry case for 6–8 servings
Fat content per serving 16 g
Energy content per serving 255 kilocalories

ROLLED OAT PASTRY

This is a variation on a basic shortcrust pastry. It is not possible to roll it out as you would with ordinary pastry – it is too crumbly – but it can be pressed into flan tins, pie dishes, and so on.

> *8 oz (225 g) rolled or porridge oats*
> *6 tablespoons rapeseed oil*
> *pinch of salt if required*
> *water to mix*

Place the oats into a mixing bowl. Make a well in the middle and add the oil and salt. Fork the ingredients through until they are well mixed and resemble bread-crumbs. Add a little water and mix to a soft dough. Press into a flan dish. Bake blind in a preheated oven, gas mark 6 (200°C, 400°F), for 15 minutes.

Makes a pastry case for 6–8 servings
Fat content per serving 19 g
Energy content per serving 306 kilocalories

CRUMBLE TOPPING

> *8 oz (225 g) rolled or porridge oats*
> *3 oz (75 g) soft brown or muscovado sugar*
> *6 tablespoons rapeseed oil*
> *1 teaspoon sesame seeds*

Place the oats, sugar and oil in a mixing bowl, in that order, and fork through until the mixture has a sticky consistency. Spread on top of the cooked fruit filling of your choice, sprinkle on the sesame seeds and bake in a preheated oven, gas mark 5 (190°C, 375°F), for 25–30 minutes.

Makes enough topping for 6 servings
Fat content per serving 19 g
Energy content per serving 340 kilocalories

TEA BREADS

Tea breads are a cross between a cake and a bread. They are invariably baked in a loaf tin, and are often sliced and served with butter on them. They usually contain a lot of dried fruit, and in the case of the tea breads below are moist enough not to need anything spread on them once sliced.

GYPSY TEABREAD

10 oz (275 g) self-raising flour
4 oz (100 g) dark brown sugar
6 oz (150 g) sultanas
2 oz (50 g) chopped mixed peel
1/2 teaspoon ground ginger
1/2 teaspoon ground cinnamon
6 oz (150 g) treacle or golden syrup
2 tablespoons skimmed milk
1 egg
1/4 teaspoon bicarbonate of soda dissolved in 2 teaspoons skimmed milk

Mix the flour, sugar, sultanas, mixed peel, ground ginger and ground cinnamon together in a mixing bowl.

In a small saucepan warm the treacle or golden syrup and the milk (this mixture should not be hot). Add the egg and whisk together. Pour this mixture into the dry ingredients in the bowl and stir well together. Add the bicarbonate of soda in milk to the mixture, stir well and pour into a 1-lb (450-g) loaf tin lined with greaseproof paper. Bake in a preheated oven, gas mark 4 (180°C, 350°F), for one hour. Remove from the oven and allow to cool for 10 minutes. Turn the tea bread out on to a wire rack to cool completely. Remove the greaseproof paper when cold.

Makes 16 slices
Fat content per slice 1 g
Energy content per slice 143 kilocalories

BARM BRACK
This simple tea bread has a delicious rich taste because of the tea in which the dried fruit is steeped.

> *7 oz (200 g) dark brown or muscovado sugar*
> *12 oz (350 g) mixed dried fruit*
> *³/₄ pint (450 ml) cold tea*
> *1 egg*
> *10 oz (275 g) self-raising flour*

Combine the sugar and dried fruit with the cold tea in a bowl. Leave to soak for at least six hours, and preferably overnight.

Beat the egg in a bowl, add the flour and the tea/sugar/fruit mixture, and stir until smooth.

Line a 1-lb (450-g) loaf tin with greaseproof paper, pour in the mixture and bake in a preheated oven, gas mark 4 (180°C, 350°F), for 1³/₄ hours. Let the bread cool in the tin for 10 minutes before turning it out on to a wire rack. Remove the greaseproof paper when quite cold.

Makes 16 slices
Fat content per slice 0.5 g
Energy content per slice 140 kilocalories

APPLE AND BANANA TEABREAD

    8 oz (225 g) peeled bananas, mashed
    8 oz (225 g) apples, peeled, cored and grated
    2 oz (50 g) sunflower seeds
    4 oz (100 g) sultanas
    4 oz (100 g) rolled oats
    2 oz (50 g) oat bran
    2 oz (50 g) wholemeal flour
    1/2 teaspoon almond essence
    4 fl oz (100 ml) mono-unsaturated or polyunsaturated
      oil

Stir all the ingredients together in a mixing bowl and turn into a 1-lb (450-g) loaf tin lined with greaseproof paper. Bake for one hour in a preheated oven, gas mark 5 (190°C, 375°F). Let the teabread cool in the tin for 10 minutes before turning it out on to a wire rack. Remove the greaseproof paper when quite cold.

Makes 12 slices
Fat content per slice 12 g
Energy content per slice 204 kilocalories

APRICOT AND OAT BRAN LOAF

    3 oz (75 g) oat bran
    8 oz (225 g) dried apricots, chopped
    4 oz (100 g) muscovado or dark brown sugar
    1 tablespoon clear honey
    grated rind of 1 lemon
    1/2 pint (300 ml) skimmed milk
    6 oz (175 g) self-raising flour
    1 teaspoon baking powder

In a bowl mix together the oat bran, chopped apricots, sugar, honey, grated lemon rind and milk. Cover and leave to stand overnight. Stir in the flour and the baking powder and mix well.

    Pour the mixture into a loaf tin that has been lined with

greaseproof paper and bake in a preheated oven, gas mark 5 (190°C, 375°F), for 1–1½ hours. Allow to cool in the tin for 10 minutes before turning out on to a wire rack. Remove the greaseproof paper when quite cold. This loaf is best kept for one or two days before serving. Store in an airtight container.

Makes 16 slices
Fat content per slice 0.6 g
Energy content per slice 134 kilocalories

SCONES

These scones and drop scones can be eaten at teatime, at breakfast or at lunch, with all sorts of low-fat toppings and spreads.

SCONES
Have these scones without any fat spread, simply served with honey or jam; or include 2 oz (50 g) of chopped dates or sultanas in the recipe.

> *8 oz (225 g) wholemeal flour*
> *1 teaspoon cream of tartar*
> *1 teaspoon bicarbonate of soda*
> *1½ oz (40 g) margarine high in polyunsaturates*
> *¼ pint (150 ml) skimmed milk or ¼ pint skimmed milk and virtually fat-free yoghurt beaten together*

Sift together the flour, cream of tartar and the bicarbonate of soda in a large bowl. Rub the margarine into the flour, then slowly add the skimmed milk or milk and yoghurt, mixing to make a soft dough. Roll out on a floured surface to half an inch (1 cm) thick and cut into 2-inch (5-cm) rounds. Place on a baking tray and bake in a preheated oven, gas mark 8 (230°C, 450°F), for about 10 minutes.

Makes 12 scones
Fat content per scone 3 g
Energy content per scone 86 kilocalories

DROP SCONES

As with ordinary scones, these can be served at any meal, warm or cold, with or without toppings, although if you are going to serve them with a topping, sweet spreads are preferable.

8 oz (225 g) self-raising flour
½ teaspoon bicarbonate of soda
1 teaspoon cream of tartar
1 tablespoon caster sugar
2 teaspoons clear honey
1 egg, beaten
¼ pint (150 ml) skimmed milk

Sift the flour, bicarbonate of soda and cream of tartar into a mixing bowl. Stir in the sugar, then add the honey, the beaten egg and the milk. Beat to a smooth batter.

Heat a heavy clean frying pan and wipe with a piece of kitchen paper dampened with mono-unsaturated/polyunsaturated oil. Drop dessertspoonfuls of the batter on to the pan. Cook until bubbles appear on the surface of the drop scones, flip them over with a spatula and cook on the other side for no more than a minute.

Makes 20–30 drop scones
Fat content per scone 0.5 g
Energy content per scone 48 kilocalories

CAKES

APPLE AND SESAME SEED CAKE

8 oz (225 g) wholemeal flour
2 teaspoons baking powder
1 tablespoon sesame seeds, toasted
4 oz (100 g) margarine high in polyunsaturates
6 oz (175 g) muscovado sugar
8 oz (225 g) finely grated and peeled apple

In a large mixing bowl combine the flour, baking powder and sesame seeds. In a saucepan set over a gentle heat and melt the margarine and sugar together. Pour this into a well in the middle of the dry ingredients and stir together thoroughly. Finally stir in the grated apple, and spoon into a well-greased 8-inch (20-cm) cake tin. Cook in a preheated oven, gas mark 4 (180°C, 350°F), for 1–1 1/2 hours or until a skewer inserted into the centre comes out clean. Allow to cool in the tin before turning out on to a wire rack.

Makes 12 slices
Fat content per slice 1 g
Energy content per slice 82 kilocalories

CHOCOLATE SPONGE CAKE

> 3 eggs
> 6 oz (175 g) caster sugar
> pinch of salt
> 1/4 teaspoon vanilla essence
> 3 tablespoons water
> 3 oz (75 g) self-raising flour, sifted
> 4 tablespoons cocoa powder
> icing sugar, to serve

Break the eggs into a bowl and beat or whisk them at high speed until they are thick and pale. Slowly add the caster sugar, continuing to beat or whisk, until the mixture is a creamy colour. Scrape the mixture off the sides of the bowl to ensure even mixing. Beat in the salt, vanilla essence and water.

Sift the flour and cocoa powder over the egg mixture, one or two tablespoons at a time, carefully folding in each addition. When the flour, cocoa and egg mixture are combined, pour into a well-greased 8-inch (20-cm) cake tin and bake in a preheated oven, gas mark 5 (190°C, 375°F), for about 30 minutes or until the surface of the cake springs back when pressed lightly. Let the cake cool for a few minutes, then turn it out on to a wire rack. Dust with icing sugar before serving.

Serves 10
Fat content per serving 4 g
Energy content per serving 26 kilocalories

TRAY BAKES

Unlike biscuits, which are individual items, tray bakes are cooked in baking trays and subsequently sliced up into individual portions.

DATE SLICE

Date mixture
8 oz (225 g) stoned dates (not sugar rolled)
6 tablespoons lemon juice
Pastry
4 oz (100 g) margarine high in polyunsaturates
12 oz (350 g) porridge oats
cold water to bind

Heat the dates and lemon juice in a saucepan, mashing the mixture with a fork. Set to one side and allow to cool.

Make the pastry by rubbing the margarine into the oats and adding just enough cold water to form a dough. Press out half the dough into a baking tray, spread the cooled date mix on top, then spread the remaining pastry dough on top of the date mix. Press down firmly and bake in a preheated oven, gas mark 6 (200°C, 400°F), for 30 minutes.

Makes 16 slices
Fat content per slice 7 g
Energy content per slice 169 kilocalories

MUESLI BAKE

For this you can either use the muesli recipe on page 62 or any other type of muesli you might purchase.

> *4 oz (100 g) plain wholemeal flour*
> *8 oz (225 g) muesli*
> *3 oz (75 g) honey*
> *2 tablespoons dark brown sugar*
> *2 tablespoons skimmed milk powder*
> *4 oz (100 g) plain virtually fat-free yoghurt*
> *1 teaspoon baking powder*
> *6 tablespoons mono-unsaturated or polyunsaturated oil*

Combine all the ingredients in a mixing bowl and stir thoroughly. Pour the mixture into a greased baking tray and press it down well. Bake in a preheated oven, gas mark 5 (190°C, 375°F), for 45 minutes. Remove from the oven and allow to cool, then cut into slabs.

Makes 16 portions
Fat content per portion 7 g
Energy content per portion 140 kilocalories

BISCUITS AND BUNS

OATCAKES

These can be eaten plain, on their own, or with sweet or savoury toppings.

> *4 oz (100 g) medium oatmeal*
> *pinch of bicarbonate of soda*
> *pinch of salt*
> *1 oz (25 g) margarine high in polyunsaturates*
> *boiling water*

Combine the oatmeal, bicarbonate of soda and salt in a mixing bowl. Melt the margarine with one tablespoon of boiling water and pour into a well in the centre of the oatmeal. Mix until you have a soft dough, adding more boiling water if necessary. Roll the dough out as thin as possible on a board dusted with oatmeal. Cut into rounds with a 3-inch (7½-cm) cutter, place on a baking sheet and bake in a preheated oven, gas mark 4 (180°C, 350°F), for 20–30 minutes until the biscuits are crisp.

Makes 10 biscuits
Fat content per biscuit 3 g
Energy content per biscuit 59 kilocalories

OAT AND WALNUT BISCUITS

    4 oz (100 g) margarine high in polyunsaturates
    3 oz (75 g) soft brown sugar
    ½ teaspoon ground nutmeg
    ½ teaspoon ground cinnamon
    1 egg, beaten
    3 oz (75 g) wholemeal flour
    5 oz (150 g) porridge oats
    2 oz (50 g) sultanas
    2 oz (50 g) chopped walnuts

Place the margarine, sugar, nutmeg and cinnamon in a mixing bowl and beat with a fork until well combined. Mix in the egg, beating well. Add the flour, oats, sultanas and walnuts and fork in until well mixed.

Place tablespoon-sized blobs of the mixture on to a well-greased baking tray. Spread them out and flatten with the back of the spoon, making sure none of the biscuits touch each other. Bake in a preheated oven, gas mark 4 (180°C, 350°F) for 20 minutes. Allow the biscuits to cool briefly on the baking sheet, then transfer to a wire rack to cool thoroughly.

Makes 12–16 biscuits
Fat content per serving 10 g
Energy content per serving 194 kilocalories

FIG AND NUT BUNS

2 oz (50 g) oatmeal
2 oz (50 g) wholemeal flour
3 oz (75 g) oatbran
3 oz (75 g) chopped walnuts
3 oz (75 g) chopped de-stalked dried figs
2 tablespoons soft brown sugar
2 teaspoons baking powder
¼ pint (150 ml) skimmed milk
1 egg
2 tablespoons mono-unsaturated or polyunsaturated oil

Place the oatmeal, wholemeal flour, oatbran, walnuts, figs, sugar and baking powder in a mixing bowl and combine thoroughly. In a separate bowl beat together the milk, egg and oil. Pour this mixture into a well in the middle of the dry ingredients and mix to a batter. Pour into deep well-greased patty tins and bake in a preheated oven, gas mark 6 (200°C, 400°F), for 20 minutes. Allow to cool in the tins for a few minutes, then turn out on to a wire rack to cool completely.

Makes 12 buns
Fat content per bun 8 g
Energy content per bun 144 kilocalories

13

START TODAY

A WEEK'S MENU

It will be obvious by now that a low-fat diet need not be a
dull one. To give you some idea of how tasty and interesting such a diet can be, we have drawn up a very simple
menu list for a week's meals. You can either follow the
programme right through one week, or pick and choose
the ideas that appeal to you.

MONDAY

Breakfast   Oat cereal and skimmed milk
                Wholemeal toast, low-fat spread and jam,
                   honey or marmalade
Lunch   Rice cakes
                Low-fat cheese, hard or soft
                Tomatoes and onion, finely chopped
                Apple
Dinner   Chilli con carne, made with lean meat
                Brown rice, boiled
                Green salad
                Virtually fat-free yoghurt

TUESDAY

Breakfast   Bran flakes and small banana, chopped

	Skimmed milk
Lunch	Pasta shell salad, made with wholemeal pasta, red and green peppers, onions, chickpeas, kidney beans, tomatoes and lean diced ham
	Wholemeal roll with a little low-fat spread
Dinner	Chicken casserole, made with chicken pieces with skin removed
	Boiled potatoes in their skins
	Lemon sorbet

WEDNESDAY

Breakfast	Oat bran cereal with skimmed milk and stewed apple
	Wholemeal toast with low-fat spread
Lunch	Baked beans on wholemeal toast
	Virtually fat-free yoghurt
	Orange
Dinner	Grilled kipper
	Tomatoes, peas and boiled potatoes in their skins
	Banana

THURSDAY

Breakfast	Porridge made from porridge oats and oat bran, with skimmed milk
	Stewed apple on top
Lunch	Wholemeal sandwich, roll or bap with low-fat spread
	Salad filling consisting of, for example, lettuce, low-fat soft cheese, tomatoes, onion, pepper, mustard and cress
	Fruit with virtually fat-free fromage frais
Dinner	Bolognese sauce made with lean mince, tomato purée, onions, grated carrot, pinch of mixed herbs, on top of wholemeal spaghetti
	Virtually fat-free yoghurt

FRIDAY

Breakfast Oat bran cereal with skimmed milk

Wholemeal toast, low-fat spread and marmalade, jam or honey

Lunch Rice salad made with tuna chunks, onions, red kidney beans, peppers, lettuce, all mixed with plain virtually fat-free fromage frais

Rye bread, crispbread or high-fibre crackers and low-fat spread

Virtually fat-free yoghurt

Dinner Cauliflower in low-fat cheese sauce, topped with toasted wholemeal breadcrumbs

Boiled carrots and jacket baked potatoes

Date slice

SATURDAY

Breakfast Porridge made with oats and oat bran, with skimmed milk and topped with a small chopped banana

Lunch Ratatouille with jacket baked potato, brown rice or wholemeal pasta

Apple or orange

Dinner Vegetable quiche (a small portion)

Mixed salad, with no dressing or a little olive oil dressing

Wholemeal bread and low-fat spread

Rice pudding made with skimmed milk

SUNDAY

Breakfast Virtually fat-free plain yoghurt, fromage frais or cottage cheese

Wholemeal toast with low-fat spread and marmalade, jam, honey or yeast extract

Lunch Lean roast meat, visible fat removed

Jacket potato or boiled potatoes in their skins

	Lightly steamed or boiled green vegetables

Lightly steamed or boiled green vegetables
Oat-topped fruit crumble with virtually fat-free yoghurt

Supper   Wholemeal sandwich with low-fat cream cheese and banana filling
Apple or orange

SHOPPING LIST

To cook or prepare the meals in the week's menu list above you will need to buy the items on the shopping list below. As well as being essential for the meals we have outlined, this list will also give you an idea of the sort of items you ought to be buying if you are on a low-fat diet. And remember, these are just basics; once you get used to cooking low-fat meals you will be able to add extensively to both the menu above and the shopping list.

- Skimmed milk
- Low-fat spread
- Pure sunflower oil margarine, or one labelled high in polyunsaturates
- Natural and fruit virtually fat-free yoghurts
- Virtually fat-free fromage frais
- Very low-fat cottage cheese
- Low-fat hard and soft cheeses
- Eggs (to be used sparingly) or egg replacer
- Olive oil (or another oil high in mono-unsaturates)
- Very lean minced beef
- Meat for roasting – very lean, with visible fat removed
- Lean ham
- Kipper, or other oily fish, e.g. smoked mackerel
- Tinned tuna
- Wholemeal flour
- Cornflour
- Oat bran
- Rolled oats
- Bran flakes

- Oat cereal
- Brown rice
- Pudding rice
- Wholewheat pasta
- Wholemeal/high-fibre bread and rolls/baps
- Rye bread/high-fibre crispbread/crackers
- Rice cakes
- Fresh/frozen vegetables
- Baking potatoes
- Salad ingredients
- Tinned tomatoes
- Dried/tinned chickpeas and red kidney beans
- Baked beans
- Tomato purée
- Dried/fresh herbs
- Apples for stewing
- Other fresh fruit, including lemons and bananas
- Dried fruit, e.g. raisins, dates, apricots
- Caster sugar
- Honey
- Jams/marmalades
- Yeast extract, e.g. Marmite

SUITABLE LOW-FAT FOODS

On the following four pages is a chart specially constructed for those wishing to adopt or cook for a low-fat diet. In the first column are listed the sort of items that can be regularly eaten without any worries, while in the last column we have listed the items at the other extreme – the high-fat foods that you should positively avoid. In between are two columns showing foods that can be eaten occasionally and foods that can be eaten for special treats; how frequently items from these two middle columns can be chosen rather depends on how much weight you want to lose and/or by how much you want to protect yourself and your family against the risk of heart disease.

A LOW-FAT DIET

Food group	Eat regularly[1]	Eat in moderation, occasionally[2]	Eat in moderation, special treats[3]	Avoid eating[4]
Cereal food	Wholemeal flour Oatmeal Wholemeal bread Whole grain cereals Porridge oats Crispbreads Brown rice Wholemeal pasta Cornmeal Untoasted sugar-free muesli	White bread White flour White rice and pasta Water biscuits	Sugar-coated cereals Plain semi-sweet biscuits Ordinary bought museli	Sweet biscuits Cream-filled biscuits Cream crackers Cheese biscuits Croissants
Fruit and vegetables	All fresh, frozen and dried fruit Unsweetened tinned fruit All fresh, frozen, dried and tinned vegetables, especially peas, baked beans, broad beans and lentils Baked potatoes (eat the skin).	Olives Oven chips labelled 'cooked in sunflower oil and 40% less fat' (grill if possible)	Fruit in syrup Crystallised fruit Avocado Chips and roast potatoes cooked in suitable oil	Deep-fat fried chips, roast potatoes Crisps and savoury snacks

188

Nuts	Walnuts Chestnuts		Peanuts and most other nuts, e.g. almonds, hazelnuts, Brazil nuts	Coconut
Fish	All fresh and frozen fish, e.g. cod, plaice, herring, mackerel Tinned fish in brine or tomato sauce, e.g. sardine, tuna	Fish fried in suitable oil	Prawns, lobster, crab Molluscs, oysters, winkles Tinned fish in oil (drained)	Fish roe Taramasalata Fried scampi
Meat	Chicken, turkey Veal Rabbit Game Soya-protein meat substitute Very lean red meat, small portion, no more than once daily	Lean beef and lamb Lean pork, ham, gammon Very lean minced meat	Liver, kidney, tripe, sweetbreads Grilled back bacon	Sausages Luncheon meats, corned beef Meat pâté, salami Streaky bacon Duck, goose, meat pies and pasties, Scotch eggs Visible fat on meats, crackling, chicken skin
Eggs and dairy foods	Skimmed milk Powdered skimmed milk Soya milk Low-fat curd cheese Virtually fat-free yoghurt Egg white Virtually fat-free fromage frais	Semi-skimmed milk No more than 3 whole eggs per week including those in baked items, e.g. cakes, quiche, flans	Medium-fat cheeses, e.g. Edam, Gouda, Camembert, Brie Cheese spreads Half-fat cheeses labelled 'low-fat' Sweetened condensed skimmed milk	Whole milk and cream Full-fat yoghurt Cheese, e.g. Cheddar, Stilton, cream cheese Evaporated or condensed milk Imitation cream Excess eggs, i.e. more than 4 per week

A LOW-FAT DIET *Continued*

Food group	Eat regularly[1]	Eat in moderation, occasionally[2]	Eat in moderation special treats[3]	Avoid eating[4]
Fats and oils	Small amounts only – see next column	Margarine and shortening labelled 'High in polyunsaturates' or 'mono-unsaturates' Low-fat spreads		All margarines, shortenings, oils not labelled 'High in polyunsaturates' or 'mono-unsaturates'
		Corn oil, sunflower oil, soya oil, safflower oil, grapeseed oil, olive oil, peanut (groundnut) oil, rapeseed oil		All spreads not labelled low-fat Butter Lard, suet, dripping Vegetable oil or margarine of unknown origin
Prepared foods	Jelly (low sugar) Sorbet Fat-free homemade soups Virtually fat-free low-sugar yoghurt Virtually fat-free natural yoghurt	Pastry, puddings, cakes, biscuits, sauces, etc., made with wholemeal flour and fat/oil as above Salad dressing made with suitable oil as above	Packet soups	Pastries, puddings, cakes and sauces made with whole milk and/or fat/ oil as above. Suet dumplings/puddings Salad dressing made with unsuitable oil Ice cream Cream soups

Sweets, preserves, jams and spreads	Marmite, Bovril Chutneys, pickles Sugar-free artificial sweeteners	Fish/meat pastes Peanut butter Low-sugar jams and marmalades	Boiled sweets Fruit pastilles and jellies Jam, marmalade Honey	Chocolate spreads Chocolates, toffees, fudge, butterscotch Carob chocolate Coconut bars
Drinks	Freshly made tea, coffee (not too many, not too strong).	Alcohol	Sweetened drinks Squashes, fruit juices Malted milk or hot chocolate drinks made with skimmed milk	Whole milk drinks Cream-based liqueurs
Sauces and dressings	Herbs and spices Tabasco, Worcestershire and soy sauces Lemon juice	Homemade dressings made with suitable oils	Low-fat or low-calorie bought mayonnaise and dressings Parmesan cheese	Ordinary or cream dressings and mayonnaises

Note: If you are overweight, foods high in sugar should be avoided and intake of suitable fats and oils should be strictly limited.
1 Eat regularly, i.e. choose from this group daily.
2 Eat in moderation, occasionally, i.e. eat moderate amounts from this group two or three times a week.
3 Eat in moderation, special treats, i.e. eat from this group once a week or less.
4 Avoid completely, especially if discovered to have hyperlipidaemia.

It should be said that, as with the week's menu and shopping list, such a chart is only a starting point for change, and it is important to realise that such changes can rarely be made overnight. First you need to be aware of and accept the need for change; until that is acknowledged, modifications to the diet are likely to be slight and transient. However, once you have accepted that change is necessary you are halfway there; you will start to experiment, and will start to seek out alternative products and foods.

It is also essential to realise that a low-fat diet is neither bland nor boring, is not time-consuming in its preparation, and can be very interesting.

FURTHER TIPS

Cutting out the butter

What are you supposed to do about the butter, margarine or spread you put on bread, toast and rolls? The simple answer, if you're trying to stick to a low-fat diet, is do without them. This might sound a little spartan, but ask yourself this: To what extent are you using butter or a soft spread because you really can't stand the taste of bread or toast without them? How much is it merely down to habit and because it would look out of the ordinary if you put marmalade or a sandwich filling straight on to the toast or bread? A lot of it is social conditioning. In fact you might find the taste of a sandwich without butter or a soft spread perfectly acceptable.

However, if you can't handle this idea, do try to switch over to a very-low-fat soft spread. But remember, you can't use these spreads for cooking or baking – they just separate when heated; indeed, they sometimes separate even on hot toast (just allow your toast to cool down before spreading). For cooking and baking you will have to use one of the margarines labelled 'low in saturates' instead, or try using a mono-unsaturated oil, as suggested on page 44.

Meat

- When cooking red meat, always trim off as much fat as possible.
- Roast joints of meat should always be cooked on a rack/cooking tray to allow any fat to drain away.
- When cooking chicken or turkey, remove the skin before cooking, and wrap the bird in foil in order to prevent the breast meat drying out.
- You can bake, roast, grill or fry meat slowly without any added fat, allowing its own juices to do the job. When cooked slowly in this way it won't dry up or go tough.
- When cooking with mince, dry-fry it to begin with, i.e. without any fat or oil. You will be surprised at how much fat the mince generates, which can then be poured off. Alternatively, boil up the mince with some cold water, then pour off the water. The mince can then be used in the recipe in the usual way.
- When cooking casseroles, stews, chilli con carne, spaghetti sauces, meat pie fillings and so on, reduce the amount of meat that's in the recipe and add a can of ready-prepared beans or pulses, e.g. red kidney beans, butter beans or chickpeas. This cuts back on the fat content, increases the complex carbohydrate content, and is cheaper.
- If you're making a stew or casserole you can reduce the fat content even further by making it a day in advance, then skimming off the fat once it has cooled – either use a spoon or spatula, or pull a paper towel across the surface if the fat is still warm.

Fish

- White fish can simply be baked in the oven, without the requirement of a rich sauce. Just brush the fish lightly with a little pure vegetable oil before putting it in the oven.
- Oily fish can be grilled slowly, without the need to add any extra fat. This applies equally well to kippers and other smoked fish.

- Another way to bake fish is to wrap it, either filleted or merely deheaded and gutted, in aluminium foil, along with some slices of tomàto and onion and a few herbs. Then place it in a hot oven for about half an hour so that it cooks in its own juices.

Sauces

- A sauce based on a roux of flour and butter or hard margarine mixed with milk is very high in fat. A low-fat alternative can be made using skimmed milk and cornflour to thicken it.
- If you use a low-fat hard cheese to flavour such a sauce, add $^1/_2$ teaspoon of Dijon mustard to bring out the flavour.
- Custard can be made with custard powder and skimmed milk to reduce the fat content. If it tastes too thin try adding extra dried skimmed milk powder.

Eating out

When you are eating out it is harder to control what you are eating, simply because you don't know what's gone into the dishes. However, as you become more aware of the foods that contain high and low levels of fat, you will become more discerning in your choice of restaurants and the dishes they serve. Here are a few guidelines, though:

- Go for simple starters, such as chilled fruit juice, melon cocktail, clear soups, salads with no dressing or only a small amount of olive oil dressing, and seafood dishes without sauces.
- Main courses might include fish, poultry, lean meat and vegetarian dishes, but try and avoid anything that has a sauce or gravy to it.
- Choose jacket or boiled potatoes rather than chips, and fresh vegetables, without sauces or butter, or, again, a salad without a dressing.
- For dessert go for a fresh fruit salad, or just fresh fruit, a sorbet or a water ice. Avoid the sundaes and confections topped with cream, sauces and chopped nuts.

- On the cheeseboard go for the lower fat cheeses such as Edam, Camembert and Brie. Eat them with water biscuits or oatmeal biscuits, and don't use butter on the biscuits.
- Avoid cream liqueurs and so-called 'connoisseur' coffees topped with cream.
- If you can't take your tea or coffee black, ask for skimmed milk or, at the very least, milk – don't accept cream.

Eating out must remain a pleasure, not a nightmare. It's no fun watching your friends tucking into dishes rich with creamy sauces while you nibble a limp lettuce salad. Choose your restaurant wisely and be aware of what you're eating, and you will be able to eat meals as exciting as anyone else's. And don't be afraid to ask your waitress or waiter about what goes into various dishes, how they are cooked or whether they can be served without a sauce.

14

CONCLUSION

In this book we have done two things:

- We have pointed out the need for many people to adopt a low-fat diet, either because they wish or need to lose weight, or because they wish or need to lower their risks of heart disease. Often these needs go hand in hand.
- We have also shown that a low-fat diet does not mean bland, boring and insubstantial meals.

Maybe you have bought this book because you are already trying to change your diet; if so, we hope the range of recipes we have given will encourage you to continue with your efforts, and will add to the meals you have already devised.

If you are merely wondering what a low-fat diet really is, then by now you should have realised that it is soundly based on common sense. It is not a diet that will leave you feeling permanently hungry; it will fill you up; it will go a long way towards helping you achieve your ideal weight; and it will help you in your efforts to reduce your risk of heart disease.

Eating should always be a pleasure. With the recipes in this book, it should remain a pleasure while at the same time helping to contribute towards a healthier life.

THE FAMILY
HEART
ASSOCIATION

The Family Heart Association (FHA) was originally founded in 1984 by two young mothers who had inherited familial hypercholesterolaemia (FH). This condition causes dangerously high levels of cholesterol in the blood and greatly increases the chances of having a heart attack at a young age. Far too few people were aware of the existence of FH and the devastating consequences it can have, so the FHA worked:

- To inform and support those affected by FH and other inherited hyperlipidaemias.
- To increase awareness of inherited hyperlipidaemias amongst the medical profession and the public.
- To encourage and support research into the causes and treatment of these conditions.

The FHA encourages those with a family history of heart attacks to ask their GPs for a blood test to check their cholesterol levels. If the blood cholesterol level is found to be raised, the most important initial treatment is to adopt a healthy diet, with foods low in saturated (animal) fats and high in fibre. To this end, the FHA can supply dietary guidance and other publications.

Since these early days, public awareness of the links between diet and heart disease has increased, and the FHA's aims have now widened, as has its structure. It is now a national charity whose membership includes both those with any form of familial hyperlipidaemia and others who are in any way worried about raised blood cholesterol levels. Currently the FHA is exploring ways in which it might respond positively to the growing public demand for cholesterol screening, and it has devised various schemes.

For more details about the FHA, about its publications and about its screening services, contact:

The Family Heart Association
9 West Way
Botley
Oxford OX2 0JB
tel: 0865 798969

USEFUL ADDRESSES

UK
Family Heart Association
9 West Way
Botley
Oxford OX2 0JB

British Heart Foundation
102 Gloucester Place
London W1H 4DH

Chest, Heart and Stroke Association
Tavistock House North
Tavistock Square
London WC1H 9JE

Chest, Heart and Stroke Association, Scottish Branch
65 North Castle Street
Edinburgh EH2 3LT

Northern Ireland Chest, Heart and Stroke Association
21 Dublin Road
Belfast BT2 7FJ

AUSTRALIA
National Heart Foundation of Australia
National Office
PO Box 2
WODEN ACT 2606

IRELAND
Irish Heart Foundation
4 Clyde Road
Ballsbridge
Dublin 4

UNITED STATES
American Heart Association
National Center
7320 Greenville Avenue
Dallas
Texas 75231

National Cholesterol Education Program
National Heart, Lung and Blood Institute
National Institutes of Health
C-200
Bethesda
Maryland 20892

INDEX

alcohol, 21, 27, 40–1

almonds: apricot and almond rice pudding, 102; spinach, cheese and almond salad, 162

amino acids, 8

angina, 25

apples: apple and banana teabread, 175; apple and sesame seed cake, 177–8; pheasant and apple, 121; pork and apple casserole, 100; red cabbage salad, 169–70; shrimp and apple surprise, 85–6; spicy cabbage, 153–4

apricots: apricot and almond rice pudding, 102; apricot and oat bran loaf, 175–6; pigeon breasts with apricots, 120

atherosclerosis, 14, 24, 25, 26–7

aubergines: aubergine sauce, 116–17; aubergines in tomato sauce, 156–7; ratatouille, 152–3; vegetable stuffed

aubergines, 124–5

avocado dip, 118

bacon, tomato and mushroom, 66

baked beans: Boston baked beans, 89–90; ham and baked beans, 66

baking, 57, 171–82

bananas: apple and banana teabread, 175; baked Caribbean bananas, 130; banana chutney, 77–8; Brie and banana salad, 170

barley, 49; barley, vegetable and yoghurt bake, 146–7

barm brack, 174

beans, 35, 49–50: bean burgers, 70; beany salad, 159–60

beef: beef curry, 99; Bolognese sauce, 138–9; herby steaks, 123–4; lean burgers, 69; ragu, 139–40; stewed beef with vegetables and lentils, 100–1

beetroot and grapefruit salad, 161–2

mushroom bake, 97–8; mushroom sauce, 136–7; mushrooms and garlic in yoghurt, seafood sauce, 137–8; stuffed mushrooms, 119

mussels, 114; mussels in white wine, 114–15

nervous system, 14

nuts, 191; baked nut risotto, 125; vegetarian nut pâté, 86–7

oats, 36, 49, 62; apricot and oat bran loaf, 175–6; date slice, 179; fresh fruit oat cocktail, 129–30; muesli bake, 180; oat and walnut biscuits, 181; oatcakes, 180–1; porridge, 63; red bean loaf, 90–1; rolled oat pastry, 172

offal, 32

oils, 9, 31–2, 42–4, 192

oleic acid, 11

olive oil, 11, 31–2

onions: baked potatoes and onion, 151; chicken breasts with spring onions, 121–2

organic fruit and vegetables, 51

organically-farmed meat, 47–8

Oriental salad, 162–3

overweight, 19–21, 38–9

packed lunches, 79–80

pancakes, 68, 107

parsnips: grated parsnip and carrot, 156

pasta, 134–40; fruit pasta salad, 159

pastry: rolled oat pastry, 172; shortcrust, 171–2

pâtés: smoked mackerel, 118–19; vegetarian nut, 86–7

peanut oil, 32, 43, 44

peanuts: brown rice and peanut salad, 158

peas: rich lentil and split pea soup, 82–3

pepper, 52

peppers: Bulgar wheat salad, 164; ratatouille, 152–3; sweetcorn and pepper salad, 160

pheasant and apple, 121

pickles, 76–8

pigeon breasts with apricots, 120

pilaff, rice, 141–2

poaching, 57–8

polyunsaturated fats, 11–12, 31, 32, 33, 42–4

pork: Boston baked beans, 89–90; haslet, 71; pork and apple casserole, 100

porridge, 63

pot-roasting, 57

potatoes, 149–51; baked potatoes and onion, 151; boiled potatoes, 149–50; cauliflower and potato in yoghurt, 155–6; jacket potatoes, 150; mashed potatoes, 150; potato cakes, 72; potato salad, 166–7; roast potatoes, 150–1; smoked fish cottage pie, 91–2

prawns: cauliflower and prawn bombe, 113–14 see also shrimps

presentation of food, 59–60

preserves, 193

206

207

More books from Optima ...

POSITIVE HEALTH GUIDES

Positive Health Guides: 'A series that gives health education a good name.' *British Medical Journal*

THE HEALTHY HEART DIET BOOK by Professor Jim Mann and Roberta Longstaff

Coronary heart disease continues to be one of the commonest causes of death and ill-health in the Western world.

Preventing heart disease is possible and particularly through a low-fat, high-fibre diet. In The Healthy Heart Diet Book Professor Jim Mann and dietician Roberta Longstaff have combined their expertise to provide up-to-date information and 140 recipes. The Oxford Diet, serialised in the Daily Mail, was based on this book.

Changing to a healthier diet and preventing coronary heart disease need not be difficult or boring, as this comprehensive and well-illustrated book ably demonstrates.

ISBN 14488 7
Price (in UK only) £5.99

CHOLESTEROL by David Symes and the FHA

High cholesterol levels are a major risk factor in the development of coronary heart disease, one of the leading killers throughout the developed world. Published with the British Family Heart Association, this book:
- explains what cholesterol is
- shows how it is linked to heart disease
- tells you how to reduce your cholesterol level
- identifies other risk factors

Practical suggestions of simple ways to improve your diet and change your lifestyle for the better make essential reading for anyone concerned about living a long and healthy life.

The Family Heart Association is a charity helping the public, industry and the medical profession to fight heart disease.

ISBN 0 356 18841 8
Price (in UK only) £3.50

BEAT HEART DISEASE! by Professor Ristéard Mulcahy

Coronary heart disease and stroke are widespread diseases whose incidence can be drastically reduced – simply by adopting a healthier lifestyle.

Professor Mulcahy – a leading cardiologist – identifies the causes, key risk factors and typical danger signs, and shows how to get back to enjoying life after a heart attack. Practical suggestions on how to modify your diet, change your lifestyle and take more exercise will not only help keep your heart healthy but bring you a happier – and longer – life.

'A splendid book to recommend to patients.' *British Medical Journal*

ISBN 0 356 19670 4
Price (in UK only) £5.99

DR ANDERSON'S HCF DIET by Dr James Anderson

Dr Anderson has proved scientifically that his High Carbohydrate and Fibre Diet can:

- help you lose weight without feeling hungry
- lower your cholesterol level by 30 per cent
- lower high blood pressure by 10 per cent

With calorie-controlled meal plans and over 140 appetising recipes, the HCF diet will help you to cut down on fat, sugar and salt. Follow this revolutionary way of staying fit and healthy – and still enjoy your food.

'Genuine scientific work ...' *Observer*

ISBN 0356 14480 1
Price (in UK only) £5.99

THE LOW-SALT DIET BOOK by Dr Graham MacGregor

Reduce your salt intake – and improve your health!

High blood pressure – linked to a high intake of salt – is one of the most preventable causes of death in the Western World.

Christiane and Graham MacGregor, well-known experts in the field of blood pressure, explain how easy it is to avoid eating, and cooking with, salt, and show how this may help to reduce high blood pressure.

85 calorie-counted and sodium-assessed recipes and meal plans allow you to discover the delicious flavours of fresher and more natural low-salt food.

ISBN 0 356 19774 3
Price (in UK only) £5.99

All Optima books are available at your bookshop or newsagent, or can be ordered from the following address:

Optima, Cash Sales Department,
PO Box 11, Falmouth, Cornwall TR10 9EN

Please send cheque or postal order (no currency), and allow 60p for postage and packing for the first book, plus 25p for the second book and 15p for each additional book ordered up to a maximum charge of £1.90 in the UK.

Customers in Eire and BFPO please allow 60p for the first book, 25p for the second book plus 15p per copy for the next 7 books, thereafter 9p per book.

Overseas customers please allow £1.25 for postage and packing for the first book and 28p per copy for each additional book.